Richard Baxter

To Live is Christ

Warning and Wooing the World,
Challenging and Comforting the Church

Introduced
by
Alan C. Clifford

CHARENTON REFORMED PUBLISHING

2022

Text © The Publisher 2022

Layout © Quinta Press 2022

First published in Great Britain 2022

by Charenton Reformed Publishing

www.christiancharenton.co.uk

All rights reserved

ISBN 978–0–9929465–9–3

Typeset in Bembo MT Pro

by Quinta Press, Weston Rhyn, Oswestry, Shropshire

Printed and bound in Great Britain by Lightning Source

British Library Cataloguing in Publication Data.

A catalogue record for this book is available from the British Library.

Cover concept: A. C. Clifford, formatting by Barkers Print & Design, Attleborough, Norfolk

Cover picture: Dr Clifford's photograph of the Kidderminster statue

The Love of God to the World was the first womb where the work of Redemption was conceived, John 3: 16.
Richard Baxter's first book (*Aphorismes of Justification*, 1649)

Consider what Christ did towards the saving of souls.
He thought them worth his blood; and shall
we not think them worth our breath?

Will you not do a little, where Christ hath done so much?
The Saints' Everlasting Rest (1650)

Nothing is more indecent than a dead preacher, speaking
to dead hearers the living truths of the living God.
Baxter citation by Philip Doddridge

I preached as never sure to preach again,
And as a dying man to dying men.
Autobiography of Richard Baxter (1696)

CONTENTS

Biographical Introduction	9
Making Light of Christ	31
The Grand Question Resolved	69
Calamy on Baxter	113
Epilogue: Baxter's Christianity	145

Richard Baxter

Preface

A Christian man who, in the estimate of others, was ranked with the Prophets, the Apostles and the Church Fathers, must be extraordinary by any standard. Such was the great Puritan Richard Baxter (1615-91). More widely read than Shakespeare in his day, he is one of England's greatest Christian preachers. His extraordinary seventeenth-century ministry at Kidderminster, Worcestershire is celebrated by an appropriate local statue. A more significant monument, Baxter's nationwide influence was diffused by such still-gripping 'page turners' as *The Saints' Everlasting Rest* and *Call to the Unconverted*. His lovely hymn 'Ye holy angels bright' is still enjoyed by modern worshippers. Neither must we ignore his colourful and dramatic life as recorded in his autobiography with its exotic Latin title *Reliquiae Baxterianae*. Baxter also made a mark on English history by his courageous stand before the infamous Judge Jeffreys in 1685.

Richard Baxter is arguably the greatest of all the Puritans—a giant among giants! As a saintly, energetic, dedicated, brilliant and large-hearted servant of Christ, he is probably the most effective pastor-evangelist this country has ever known. Certainly, what C. H. Spurgeon was to the 19th, and George Whitefield (together with the Wesley brothers) was to the 18th, Baxter was to 17th century England. A. B. Grosart wrote that Baxter is said 'to have drawn more hearts to the great bleeding heart than any other Englishman of his age'.

Furthermore, his pen-productions proved just as famous as his pulpit ministry at Kidderminster. The sheer scale and variety of his contribution over a forty-two year period is breathtaking, including his late massive scholarly Latin treatise *Methodus theologiae christianae* (1681) and the earlier popular persuasive to holiness *A Saint or a Brute* (1662). Remarkably, many of Baxter's writings are still being published 300 years on. His style remains surprisingly lucid and lively when most of his contemporaries are obviously dated. Baxter's books still retain their power to inform, arouse and edify the modern reader. His message remains as powerful and meaningful as ever.

For further confirmation of this claim, this book contains the complete texts of two of Baxter's shorter, little-known and unjustly-neglected publications, the first and last of his evangelistic/pastoral works, *Making Light of Christ* (1655) and *The Grand Question Resolved* (1692).

Acknowledgements

For the type-setting, layout and production of this book I am grateful for the personal interest and professional expertise of Dr Digby James of Quinta Press. Barkers Print & Design are thanked for help with formatting the cover and the facilities provided by Lightning Source are much appreciated. The engraving of Baxter comes from my 1701 copy of his *Paraphrase on the New Testament* (1685).

Biographical Introduction[1]

A brief outline

Birth and Education

Who then was Richard Baxter? He was born at Rowton, Shropshire on 12 November 1615, returning at the age of ten to his parents' home at Eaton Constantine, 'a mile from the Wrekin Hill, and above half a mile from Severn River and five miles from Shrewsbury'.[2] His parents were godly folk yet lacking the means to educate an obviously gifted son. Young Richard was deeply influenced by the writings of puritan authors like William Perkins and Richard Sibbes. Following an early conversion, he had an immense thirst for knowledge. Although he never attended university, he probably mastered more information through the years than many a college professor!

Ordination

A private education led to ordination by the Bishop of Worcester in 1638 and a brief curacy at Bridgenorth. For all his zeal, his parishioners were a 'hard-hearted' people. A loyal son of the Church of England with nonconformist sympathies, Baxter's attachment to Puritanism was heightened by the 'Romanising' measures of Archbishop Laud. Baxter accepted an invitation to a

---

1 For overall factual usefulness, see Geoffrey F. Nuttall, *Richard Baxter* (London: Nelson, 1965).

2 Richard Baxter, *The Autobiography of Richard Baxter*, ed. J. M. Lloyd Thomas (London: J. M. Dent, 1931), 3. Hereinafter *Autobiography*.

living at Kidderminster where he was to exercise an extraordinary ministry for around sixteen years (over two periods).

Parliamentary Chaplain

With the advent of the Civil War, he supported the Parliamentary cause. His life being threatened by the Royalists of Worcestershire, he withdrew to Coventry where he became a chaplain. After the decisive Battle of Naseby (1645), Baxter served in Colonel Whalley's regiment. Unlike John Owen, he had first-hand experience of the war, being present at several battles.[1] However, he remained an observer, and was never a combatant: 'I never struck with a sword in war or peace'.[2] Yet, as a contender for Christian truth, he was to become embroiled in battles of another kind. Indeed, his experience of religious sectarianism during these years disturbed him deeply. He considered that the war had been a disaster for the Gospel. His special dread was the alarming growth of antinomianism—a stress on the doctrines of grace at the expense of practical godliness. These developments profoundly influenced Baxter's conception of the Christian life. In fact, he acknowledges he had shared some of these errors himself:

> I had ... engaged myself as a disputer against Universal Redemption ... but [when] new notions called me to new thoughts ... I went to the Scripture, where its whole current, but especially Matth. 25 did quickly satisfy me in the doctrine of Justification: and I remembered two or three things in Dr Twisse (whom I most esteemed) ... [who] ... every where professeth, that Christ so far died for all, as to purchase them Justification and Salvation, if they believe.[3]

---

[1] Tim Cooper, *John Owen, Richard Baxter and the Formation of Nonconformity* (Farnham, Surrey: Ashgate, 2011); also 'Why Did Richard Baxter and John Owen Diverge? The Impact of The First Civil War' in *The Journal of Ecclesiastical History*, 61.3 (Cambridge: CUP, 2010).

[2] *Richard Baxter's Penitent Confession* (London: 1691), 49.

[3] *Richard Baxter's Catholick Theologie* (London: 1675), Preface.

The Kidderminster Ministry

On leaving the army in 1647, Baxter was seriously ill. While convalescing at the home of Sir Thomas Rouse at Worcester, he conceived his first two books—*Aphorismes of Justification* (1649) and the *Saints Everlasting Rest* (1650). They were published soon after resuming his parish ministry. Baxter never enjoyed robust health. He says "In my labours at Kidderminster after my return I did all under languishing weakness, being seldom an hour free from pain ..."[1] But how God blessed the prayers and preaching of Richard Baxter! Although the parish church was large, five galleries were added before long. Dr D. Martyn Lloyd-Jones had no hesitation in saying of 'Baxter at Kidderminster' that 'we are entitled to speak of revival'.[2]

He published numerous books during the Kidderminster years, including the famous *Gildas Salvianus: The Reformed Pastor* (1656) and *A Call to the Unconverted* (1658). Of the *Call*, Baxter declared, "... I published this little book, which God hath blessed with unexpected success beyond all the rest that I have written (except *The Saints Rest*)."[3]

The town witnessed an astonishing spiritual and moral reformation. In Baxter's words, "On the Lord's Days there was no disorder to be seen in the streets, but you might hear an hundred families singing psalms and repeating sermons as you passed through the streets. In a word, when I came thither at first there was about one family in a street that worshipped God, and when I came away, there were some streets where there was not passed one family ... that did not so ..."[4]

Passionate Preacher

There was a heavenly unction and fervour about Baxter's preaching.

---

[1] *Autobiography*, 76.
[2] 'Revival: An Historical and Theological Survey' (Puritan Conference Report, 1959) in *The Puritans: Their Origins and Successors* (Edinburgh: The Banner of Truth Trust, 1987), 3.
[3] *Autobiography*, 96.
[4] Ibid. 79.

None could hear him without being deeply affected. Burdened for souls while gripped with persistent pain and weakness, he tells us that he preached 'as a dying man to dying men, never sure to preach again'.[1] When Baxter preached of Christ, faith, repentance, holiness, heaven and hell, his vivid and impassioned eloquence left none doubting their reality. Not surprisingly, Baxter deplored lifeless preaching: 'Nothing is more indecent than a dead preacher, speaking to dead hearers the living truths of the living God!'[2]

Protestant Unity

Baxter was not only famous for his evangelistic and pastoral work. His view of Roman Catholicism was uncompromising, yet, grieved at the sectarianism of the times, he is also remembered for his attempts to unite Protestants. Believers of all denominations regularly worshipped at Kidderminster parish church and his 'Worcestershire Association' successfully united ministers on essential gospel truths. It became a model for similar gatherings in other counties.

What then was Richard Baxter's churchmanship? As a conservative Puritan, he believed the Church of England needed further reformation. Believing that the 'old diocesan frame'[3] was 'intolerable',[4] he welcomed Parliament's reform agenda[5] and spoke warmly of the Westminster Assembly of Divines. However, he thought some of the Presbyterians—with whom he had most sympathy—too hierarchical. Independents and Baptists he thought too 'ultra' in many things. They encouraged fragmentation and pride. However, Baxter loved all true godly men, whatever their

---

1 Ibid. 79 and 281.
2 Cited in *Lectures on Preaching* in *The Works of the Rev. P. Doddridge, D. D.* ed. E. Williams and E. Parsons (Leeds: 1804), v. 461.
3 *Autobiography*, 155.
4 Ibid. 98.
5 See *The Constitutional Documents of the Puritan Revolution 1625–1660*, ed. S. R. Gardiner (Oxford: Clarendon Press, 1906), 137ff.

views about church order and baptism. Disgusted by 'party spirit', Baxter the 'mere Nonconformist' liked to call himself a 'Catholic Christian'[1] and a 'mere Christian'"[2] who would as soon be a 'martyr for love as any article of the creed.'[3] His guiding principle was *'unity in things necessary and liberty in things unnecessary, and charity in all'*.[4] It was this that justified his policy of 'occasional conformity' after 1662: his rejection of imposed Anglicanism did not imply that he thought everything Anglican was wrong. Imperfect Christians ought not to deny some degree of fellowship with other imperfect Christians, especially when the 'fundamentals' were sincerely believed and faithfully preached.[5] Nonetheless, besides irritating the puritan sects, such ideals placed Baxter on a collision course with the eventually-restored and inflexible Anglican establishment.

Authentic Calvinist

Richard Baxter also proposed a solution to the major theological division of the day, the Calvinist-Arminian debate. Published in later years, his monumental folio *Richard Baxter's Catholic Theologie* (1675) is testimony to his enduring efforts in this regard. While he believed Arminians were in error at many points, Baxter believed that *High* Calvinists like John Owen (whose antipathy to universal atonement he once shared) were guilty of an 'ultra-orthodox' over-reaction. As we have seen, the Civil War conflict and the consequent war of words had led him to a fresh examination of the Bible. So, as the Huguenot theologian Amyraut had argued in France, Baxter—aided by the views of Dr William Twisse—argued in England that, notwithstanding the truth of sovereign

---

1   Nuttall, *Richard Baxter*, 84.

2   *Autobiography*, 293.

3   Ibid. 170; also William Bates, *A Funeral Sermon* William Bates, *A Funeral Sermon for the Reverend, Holy and Excellent Divine, Mr Richard Baxter* (London: 1692), 120; also W. Bates, *The Whole Works of the Rev. W. Bates, DD*, ed. W. Farmer (London: 1815), iv. 297ff.

4   *Autobiography*, 91.

5   See *Autobiography*, ed. N. H. Keeble (London: Dent, 1974), pp. xxff.

divine election, the Scriptures taught a designed sufficiency in the death of Christ for all mankind. This double emphasis was rooted in the paradox of God's hidden purposes and his revealed promises. Besides being rigorously scriptural, he believed that his position possessed vital evangelistic and pastoral advantages. Fully endorsing the Canons of Dort, Baxter pointed out that John Calvin and several members of the Westminster Assembly also taught universal atonement. Above all, he argued his case from plain texts of the Bible:

> When God saith so expressly that Christ died for all [2 Cor. 5: 14–15], and tasted death for every man [Heb. 2: 9], and is the ransom for all [1 Tim. 2: 6], and the propitiation for the sins of the whole world [1 Jn. 2: 2], it beseems every Christian rather to explain in what sense Christ died for all, than flatly to deny it.[1]

Against Antinomianism

Baxter's response to antinomianism proved troublesome. Rightly stressing that the sinner's justification before God involves a trusting, loving and obedient faith in Christ as Prophet, Priest *and* King (thus the gospel covenant involves grace *and* law), his doctrine of justification—involving a proper understanding of faith and works—was misunderstood. Yet his apparent deviations from orthodoxy were more verbal than real. His view being sounder than Owen's, his valid emphasis on the necessity of holiness for salvation never detracted from the Reformation doctrine of salvation by grace alone through faith in Christ alone:

> I abhor the opinion of any works necessary to justification or salvation, or to any common blessings in the sense of Paul; such as make the reward to be of debt, and not of grace. I think few men living, are less tempted to magnify or trust to any worth

---

[1] See Richard Baxter, *The Universal Redemption of Mankind* (London: 1694), Joseph Read, 'To the Reader' and 286.

of their own, than I am. I look not for a bit of bread, or an hour's ease, or life, or the pardon, or acceptance of one duty, or of my holiest affections (so faulty are they by their great imperfection) but merely from the free grace of God, and the merits and intercession of Christ. ... The faith by which we are justified, is that true Christianity which includeth our believing consent to God the Father, Son, and Holy Ghost; our belief of Christ, and our thankful acceptance of him to be our Teacher, Intercessor or Priest, and King, with his offered Grace; and that this acceptance is with desire, love, and hope, expressed in a holy contract or covenant. This is the soul's marriage with Christ, and allegiance to him, and it includeth the renouncing our trust in all creatures, or in any righteousness of our own, so far as they would usurp the least part of Christ's office, works, or honour. None of all this is justification by works.[1]

Nonconformist Leader

While Baxter was sympathetic with the Parliamentary cause, he was unhappy with many features of Oliver Cromwell's Protectorate. Believing —surely not without *some* qualification—'our ancient monarchy to be a blessing and not an evil',[2] Baxter considered the Lord Protector's 'design' was 'to do good in the main, and to promote the Gospel and the interest of godliness more than any had done before him'.[3] Indeed, the preacher's ministry had flourished more under Cromwell's rule than under the Stuarts. However, in his view, the excessive religious liberty of the new order was no just alternative to the tyranny of the old. Following Oliver's death, Baxter's concern to resolve differences and promote concord continued. He dedicated his *Five Disputations of Church Government and Worship* (1659) and *A Key for Catholics* (1659) to

---

[1] Richard Baxter, *A Defence of Christ and Free Grace* (London: 1690), 'To the Reader' and 24.
[2] *Autobiography*, 140.
[3] Ibid. 70.

Richard Cromwell who, much to the chagrin of John Owen, favoured the Presbyterians and government by political consensus.

In 1660, Baxter left Kidderminster for London. He was involved in plans to restore Charles II to the throne, and he preached before Parliament at St Margaret's, Westminster. Baxter became a chaplain to the King who offered him the bishopric of Hereford. Preferring to return to his people at Kidderminster—a move which was thwarted—Baxter refused the King's offer on conscientious grounds.

Anxious to secure a just church settlement, he took a prominent part in the Savoy Conference of 1661 where he stood shoulder to shoulder with moderate Episcopalians and Presbyterians. Still uncomfortable with several unbiblical features of the *Book of Common Prayer*, Baxter contributed to the liturgical discussion by producing his *Reformed Liturgy*, written in the space of fourteen days.

The Great Ejection

However, Baxter's essential conservatism blinded him to the scheming duplicity of Charles II. Although the restored King had promised to grant religious liberty, many, including Baxter, were utterly deceived. Once it became clear that the Church of England was to be restored with all its strictness, Baxter soon realised his duty. A few months before the infamous Act of Uniformity came into effect on 24 August 1662—which led to the ejection of around 2,000 sound, godly, evangelical ministers—Baxter bid farewell to the Church of England in a sermon at Blackfriars. The inflexible and intolerant terms of the Act—deliberately framed to secure this objective—made it impossible for conscientious Bible-believing pastors to conform.[1] Re-ordination by an unbiblical episcopate and strict imposition of an anti-Puritan liturgy and lectionary

---

[1] See A. H. Drysdale, *History of the Presbyterians in England* (London: Pubication Committee of the Presbyterian Church of England, 1889), 383ff; also G. F. Nuttall, 'The First Nonconformists' in *From Uniformity to Unity*, ed. G. F. Nuttall and O. Chadwick (London: SPCK, 1962), 149ff.

were too much to stomach. Strict conformity to the Word of God was all that mattered to the courageous Nonconformists. Becoming the leading figure among the ejected clergy, Baxter's account of the 'Great Ejection' vividly portrays the pain of his brethren and their families:

> When Bartholomew Day came, about one thousand eight hundred or two thousand ministers were silenced and cast out. … And now came in the great inundation of calamities, which in many streams overwhelmed thousands of godly Christians, together with their pastors … Hundreds of able ministers, with their wives and children, had neither house nor bread … The people's poverty was so great that they were not able much to relieve their ministers …[1]

Marriage

In September 1662 Baxter married Margaret Charlton, a young woman whom he had led to Christ at Kidderminster. He was 47 and she only 23. Many tongues wagged and eyebrows were raised, for Baxter had favoured celibate self-denial in the interests of pastoral dedication. That said, he amusingly reports: 'And I think the king's marriage was scarce more talked of than mine'.[2] However, it was indeed a marriage made in heaven. The couple were ideally suited, and Margaret was to prove a great comfort and encouragement to Richard until her early death in 1681.

Published soon after his wife's death, grief-stricken Baxter's *Poetical Fragments* reveal the mystical side to his nature. Besides including the two still-popular hymns 'Ye holy angels bright' and 'Lord, it belongs not to my care', the work contains some pretty impressive poetry, bordering on the Miltonic. In the 'Epistle to the Reader', we discover his love of music:

> For myself, I confess that harmony and melody are the pleasure

---

[1] *Autobiography*, 175.
[2] Ibid. 174.

and elevation of my soul and have made a Psalm of Praise in the Holy Assembly the chief delightful exercise of my religion and my life; and hath helped to bear down all the objections which I have heard against church music, and against the 149, 150 Psalms. It was not the least comfort that I had in the converse of my late dear wife, that our first in the morning, and last in bed at night, was a Psalm of Praise, (till the hearing of others interrupted it).[1]

Evidently, the Baxters sang lustily and fervently! One also imagines how glorious the singing must have been at Kidderminster when the five added galleries were full! While we may assume the music was confined to the tunes of the metrical psalms, one wonders what Baxter might have thought in later years of the church music of Henry Purcell (1658–95). If the pompous Anglican service might have been not quite to his puritanical liking, it is difficult to imagine—had it been technically possible—he wouldn't have relished the 'pietistic' music of his near-contemporary, the German Lutheran composer Dietrich Buxtehude (1637–1707). After all, several of Baxter's works were translated into German, widely distributed and warmly appreciated.

The Plague Year

Baxter was living with his wife and mother-in-law at Acton in Middlesex when the terrible plague sent many to an early grave during the hot summer of 1665. Most of the conforming Anglicans left the city while the nonconformist pastors gloriously adorned their ordination vows, a fact Baxter justly observed:

And when the plague grew hot most of the conformable ministers fled, and left their flocks in the time of their extremity, whereupon divers Nonconformists, pitying the dying and distressed people that had none to call the impenitent to

---

[1] Richard Baxter, *Poetical Fragments: Heart Employment with God and Itself* (London: 1681), 'Preface to the Reader'.

repentance, nor to help men to prepare for another world, nor to comfort them in their terrors, when about ten thousand died in a week, resolved that no obedience to the laws of any mortal men whosoever could justify them for neglecting of men's souls and bodies in such extremities, ...[1]

Baxter and his family were preserved. The great fire of London occurred the following year, 'one judgement on the back of another' as one historian wrote. The widespread devastation included old St Paul's cathedral where, twelve years earlier (17 December 1654), Baxter had preached to the largest congregation he ever witnessed.[2] That said, he lamented the destruction of books more than buildings:

> And among the rest, the loss of books was an exceeding great detriment to the interest of piety and learning. Almost all the booksellers in St Paul's churchyard brought their books into vaults under St Paul's church, where it was thought almost impossible that fire should come. But the church itself being on fire, the exceeding weight of the stones falling down did break into the vault and let in the fire, and they could not come near to save the books.[3]

Christian Apologist

Notwithstanding these events, Baxter preached and pastored when he could. He was also busy with his books. *The Divine Life* was published in 1664, *Reasons for the Christian Religion* appeared in 1667 followed in 1670 by *A Cure of Church Divisions*. Then *More Reasons for the Christian Religion* appeared in 1672. Powicke is right to highlight Baxter's magnificent accomplishment in demonstrating the intellectual integrity of the Christian Faith. *The Reasons of the Christian Religion* 'still stands as a monument

---

[1] *Autobiography*, 196.
[2] See Nuttall, 79. It was 'the greatest congregation that ever I saw', *Sermon on Judgement* (London, 1658), Epistle dedicatory, ii.
[3] *Autobiography*, 198f.

of convincing apologetic. It was one of the first of its kind in the language, and in respect of its method, one of the best … It presents Baxter intellectually on his highest level; and is not the less impressive because of the intense emotion which, here and there, breaks through the hard crust of his argument'.[1] One may add that Baxter provided a solid foundation for Christian convictions, secure even against the subsequent pseudo-scientific assaults inspired by David Hume and Charles Darwin.

Global visionary

Baxter was not only concerned with reforming the Church, preaching the Gospel and contending for the Faith at home. His obedience to 'the Great Commission' possessed a remarkable global dimension. In view of the merciful victory against the Turks at the gates of Vienna in 1683, he was evidently aware of the implications of the Islamic threat.[2] With strikingly-prophetic significance, he expressed himself thus:

> I was wont to look but little further than England in my prayers, as not considering the state of the rest of the world. Or if I prayed for the conversion of the Jews, that was almost all. But now, as I better understood the case of the world and the method of the Lord's Prayer, so there is nothing in the world that lieth so heavy upon my heart as the thought of the miserable nations of the earth. It is the most astonishing part of all God's providence to me, that he so far forsaketh almost all the world, and confineth his special favour to so few; that so small a part of the world hath the profession of Christianity in comparison of heathens, Mahometans and other infidels … No part of my prayers are so deeply serious as that for the conversion of the infidel and ungodly world, that God's name

---

1　F. J. Powicke, *Richard Baxter Under the Cross* (London: Jonathan Cape Ltd, 1927), 66.
2　See *The Reasons of the Christian Religion* (London: 1667), 202–4.

may be sanctified and his kingdom come, and his will be done on earth as it is in heaven.[1]

Driven by his view of the Gospel, such was the thinking that led to Baxter's enthusiastic support for the work of John Eliot amongst the Indians of Massachusetts, more than a century before William Carey and Andrew Fuller commenced the era of modern missions proper.

Suffering for Christ

Baxter shared in the cruel persecution and sufferings of the Nonconformists. He was imprisoned for a week at Clerkenwell in 1669, and for nearly two years at Southwark in 1684-6, aged 70. This second term of imprisonment is associated with his trial at the hands of the notorious Judge Jeffreys, occasioned by the publication of Baxter's *Paraphrase on the New Testament* (1685). Because of certain textual comments, the author was accused of libelling the Church of England. However, at the deepest level, the real clash between Jeffreys and his puritan prey was over spirituality rather than legality. Piety was savaged by impiety. Baxter's preface probably challenged and irritated the ungodly Judge:

> Reader, I beg of you, as from Christ, for his sake, for your soul's sake, for your children's sake, for the sake of Church and Kingdom, that you will conscionably and seriously set up family religion, calling upon God, singing his praises, and instructing your children and servants in the Scripture and Catechism, and in a wise and diligent education of youth. Hear me, as if I beg'd it of you with tears on my knees. Alas, what doth the world suffer by the neglect of this! It is out of ungodly families that the world hath ungodly rulers, ungodly ministers, and a swarm of serpentine enemies of holiness and peace, and their own salvation. What country groaneth not under the confusions,

---

[1] *Autobiography*, 117.

miseries and horrid wickedness, which are all the fruits of family neglects, and the careless and ill education of youth.[1]

The trial—immortalized by Lord Macaulay[2]—was a forgone conclusion. The Lord Chief Justice wasn't very interested in truth or justice. The sick and aged Baxter was repeatedly shouted down when attempting to speak. Scurrility knew no bounds when Jeffreys abused the saintly Baxter. "This is an old rogue" cried the judge, "and hath poisoned the world with his Kidderminster doctrine!" Baxter was reviled as "an old schismatical knave, a hypocritical villain!" When further attempting to explain his views, the Lord Chief Justice burst forth, "Richard, Richard, dost thou think we'll hear thee poison the court? Richard, thou art an old fellow, an old knave; thou hast written books enough to load a cart, every one as full of sedition, I might say treason, as an egg is full of meat. Hadst thou been whipped out of thy writing trade forty years ago, it had been happy ..."[3] Such is how Christ's enemies treat his faithful servants!

Liberty to Preach

Baxter was released from prison on 24 November 1686. The Lord's aged warrior still had plenty of fight left in him, so he moved to Charterhouse Yard to assist the ministry of his friend Matthew Sylvester. More theological and devotional books flowed from his pen. Indeed, Baxter had written enough books 'to load a cart'—141 in all.[4] His penultimate offering was *The Certainty of the World of Spirits*, a work typical of the other-worldliness of one who lived and laboured that others might enjoy 'everlasting rest.'

Last Years and Death

Baxter lived to see better days. With the 'Glorious Revolution' of

---

[1] Preface to *A Paraphrase on the New Testament* (London: 1685).
[2] See Lord Macaulay, *History of England,* intr. A. G. Dickens (London: Heron Books, 1967), i. 381–5.
[3] *Autobiography*, 262.
[4] See the Baxter bibliography in Nuttall, 132ff.

1688, Protestant William and Mary ascended the throne. His hopes for 'comprehension' within the national Church being dashed, Baxter had to be content with the 'toleration' provided by the Act of 1689. Thus he continued preaching until the end. After his last sermon, he crept home to his bed, utterly exhausted. There was a glory about Baxter's last hours. To his friends Matthew Sylvester and William Bates he declared in a whisper, "I bless God I have a well grounded assurance of my eternal happiness, and great peace and comfort within."[1] When reminded of the good his books had done, the dying saint replied, "I was but a pen in the hand of God; and what praise is due to a pen?"[2] As his agonies intensified, he admitted, "I have pain, there is no arguing against sense, but I have peace, I have peace."[3] Baxter's final words were spoken to Matthew Sylvester: "The Lord teach you to die."[4] And so, on 8 December 1691, Richard Baxter entered that rest which remains for the people of God.

I close this brief outline with the slightly-edited 'eulogy' of J. M. Lloyd Thomas:

> He towered above most of even the leaders of his contemporaries, ... His physical and moral courage matched the bravest valour of his times. Earth had little to bestow on him wherewith to comfort his diseased body or console his longing soul. He looked up wistfully to the Saints' Everlasting Rest and groaned in spirit for release from his pains and the contentions of the world.[5]

---

[1] William Bates, *A Funeral Sermon*, 126.
[2] Ibid. 125.
[3] Ibid. 129.
[4] Matthew Sylvester, *Elisha's Cry after Elijah's God* (London, 1696), 17.
[5] *Autobiography*, p. xviii.

AN ELEGY

On the Death of that Learned, Pious, and Laborious minister of Jesus Christ

Mr. RICHARD BAXTER

Who departed this Mortal Life on the 8th Day of December, 1691.[1]

HOW hardly we sad doleful Truths believe!
And though prepar'd, unwillingly we grieve.
But here's a Subject calls for Floods of Tears,
For who of *Baxter*'s late Departure hears,
But is prepar'd to weep? Yet Tears are vain,
Not us they profit, nor that happy Man
Who from the Vale of Sorrows is remov'd,
Baxter so much Esteem'd, Amir'd, Belov'd;
Whose pious Words which from his Mouth did come,
Distill'd with Sweetness like the Hony-Comb,
Is silent ——Yet that Word I must recall,
Tho' Dead, *his Words yet speak unto us all.*
Who can attempt the Subject of his Praise?
All we alas ! can say, are faint essays.
But still Respect to's pious Worth is due,
We cannot flatter, but we must be true:

---

[1] These items are possibly compositions by a relative of Thomas Baldwin, one of Baxter's Kidderminster assistants. The Epitaph probably adorned Baxter's gravestone at Christ Church, Newgate. In 1924 a mural inscription was placed in the church to mark his burial there. Sadly nothing remains. The church was demolished after bomb damage in 1941.

Learn'd tho' he was with all that Human Skill,
Which empty Heads with wind too often fill,
Yet humble without Pride——his Learning he,
Still made the Handmaid to Divinity;
Those Parts which other Men so much abuse,
He still improv'd to a Religious use,
Witness his Works in which tho' learning shine,
Yet serv'd as Foils to set off Thoughts Divine.
But who his Heavenly Piety can paint?
He did not seem, but surely was a Saint:
His private Notions, though some men condemn,
Not Envy could his Life and Actions blame;
So much of Heaven in his Talk was known,
Atheists from him have with Convictions gone;
To prove the Truth some men have much time spent,
He was *Religion's Living Argument*:
For whosoe're his pious Actions knew,
He must believe Religion to be true.
If as a private Man his Graces were
So bright; what was he as a Minister?
That Holy Function he his Pleasure made,
Religion was his Business, not his Trade:
With empty Shews his God he did not mock,
He neither car'd to fleece nor starve his Flock;
Painful in Preaching, constant still in Prayer,
The good of Souls was his——his only care.
His Doctrins he so well apply'd, that all
Who came to him for help, did never fail:
To Weak gave Strength, to Scrupulous gave ease,
And Balm apply'd to wounded Consciences;
The kind Physician of the sickly Soul,
How many now in Grief his Loss condole!
Altho' we cannot reach his Graces height,
Yet lawfully we all may imitate.

The Sweets of Sin how quickly are they past!
The Godly Life brings pleasure at the last.
This Truth full well the Reverend *Baxter* knew,
Who when he died, had nothing else to do:
His peace with God was made, how few alas!
Of bright Professors are in such a Case?
If for Degrees of Grace are here attain'd,
Degrees of Glory are in Heaven gain'd.
Sure Pious *Baxter* may be thought to be,
A Star in Glory of the first Degree;
Who after a long Life of Pains and Age,
Death took him from this Frail, this Mortal Stage;
Who now in Heaven undoubtedly is blest,
With what he in his Works so well exprest,
The Saints expected *Everlasting Rest.*

EPITAPH

Consider, Reader, who lies here,
And for thy Loss then Drop a Tear;
'Tis BAXTER, whose unwearied Pen
Strove to Reform the Lives of Men:
Who Godliness and Learning joyn'd
To all the Beauties of his Mind;
Of God and of good Men belov'd;
None e'er their Talents more improv'd;
Heav'n lengthened out his Glass, that we
By him might learn true Piety:
His Soul is gone, true Bliss to find,
His body here is left behind,
And through the World the Product of his Mind.

LONDON, Printed for Richard Baldwin, MDCXCI

Making light of

CHRIST

AND

SALVATION

Too oft the Issue of gospel-Invitations.

Manifested in a SERMON preached at *Laurence Jury* in *London*.

By RICH. BAXTER, Teacher of the Church of Christ at *Kederminster* in *Worcestershire*.

Heb. 2. 34. *How shall we escape, if we neglect so great salvation?*

LONDON,
Printed by *R. White*, for *Nevil Simmons* Bookseller in *Kederminster*, 1656.

Making Light of Christ
and Salvation

TO THE READER

READER,

Being called on in London to preach, when I had no time to study, I was fain to preach some sermons that I had preached in the country a little before. This was one, which I preached at St Laurence, in the church where my reverend and faithful brother in Christ, Mr Richard Vines, is pastor: when I came home I was followed by such importunities by letters to print the sermon, that I have yielded thereunto, though I know not fully the ground of their desires. Seeing it must [go] abroad, will the Lord but bless it to the cure of thy contempt of Christ and grace, how comfortable may the occasion prove to thee and me! It is the slighting of Christ and salvation, that undoes the world. O happy man if thou escape but this sin! Thousands do split their souls on this rock which they should build them on. Look into the world, among rich and poor, high and low, young and old, and see whether it appear not by the whole scope of their conversations that they set more by something else than Christ? And for all the proclamations of his grace in the gospel, and our common professing ourselves to be his disciples, and to believe the glorious things that he hath promised us in another world, whether it yet appear not by the deceitfulness of our service, by our heartless endeavours to obtain his kingdom, and by our busy and delightful following of the world, that the most who are called Christians do yet in their hearts make light of Christ; and if so, what wonder if they perish by their contempt? Wilt thou but soberly peruse this short discourse, and consider well as thou readest of its truth and weight, till thy heart be sensible what a sin it is to make light of Christ and thy own salvation, and till the Lord that bought thee be advanced in the estimation and affections of thy soul, thou shalt hereby rejoice, and fulfil the desires of

Thy servant in the faith,
RICHARD BAXTER

MAKING LIGHT OF CHRIST AND SALVATION,

TOO OFT
THE ISSUE OF GOSPEL INVITATIONS

"But they made light of it."—Matt. xxii. 5.

THE blessed Son of God, that thought it not enough to die for the world, but would himself also be the preacher of grace and salvation, doth comprise in this parable the sum of his gospel. By the king that is here said to make the marriage is meant God the Father, that sent his Son into the world to cleanse them from their sins, and espouse them to himself. By his Son, for whom the marriage is made, is meant the Lord Jesus Christ, the eternal Son of God, who took to his Godhead the nature of man, that he might be capable of being their Redeemer when they had lost themselves in sin. By the marriage is meant the conjunction of Christ to the soul of sinners, when he giveth up himself to them to be their Saviour, and they give up themselves to him as his redeemed ones, to be saved and ruled by him; the perfection of which marriage will be at the day of judgment, when the conjunction between the whole church and Christ shall be solemnized. The word here translated *marriage,* rather signifieth the marriage-feast; and the meaning is, that the world is invited by the gospel to come in and partake of Christ and salvation, which comprehendeth both pardon, justification, and right to salvation, and all other privileges of the members of Christ. The invitation is God's offer of Christ and salvation in the gospel; the servants that invite them are the preachers of the gospel, who are sent forth by God to that end; the preparation for the feast there mentioned, is the sacrifice of Jesus Christ, and the enacting of a law of grace, and opening a way for revolting sinners to return to God. There is a mention of sending second messengers, because God useth not to take the first denial, but to exercise his patience till sinners are obstinate. The first persons invited are the Jews; upon their obstinate refusal they are sentenced to punishment: and the Gentiles are invited, and not only invited, but by powerful preaching, and miracles, and effectual grace, compelled; that is, infallibly prevailed with to come in. The number of them is so great that the house is filled with guests: many come sincerely, not only looking at the pleasure of the feast, that is, at the pardon of sin, and deliverance from the wrath of God, but also at the honour of the marriage, that is, of the Redeemer, and their profession by giving up themselves to a holy conversation: but some come in only for the feast, that is, justification by Christ, having not the wedding-garment of sound resolution for obedience in their life, and looking only at themselves in believing, and not to the glory of their Redeemer; and these are sentenced to everlasting misery, and speed as ill as those that came not in at all; seeing a faith that will not work is but like that of the devil; and they that look to be pardoned and saved by it are mistaken, as James sheweth, chap. ii. 24.

The words of my text contain a narration of the ill entertainment that the gospel findeth with many to whom it is sent, even after a first and second invitation. They made light of it, and are taken up with other things. Though it be the Jews that were first guilty, they have too many followers among us Gentiles to this day.

THE DOCTRINE OF THE PASSAGE.—For all the wonderful

love and mercy that God hath manifested in giving his Son to be the Redeemer of the world, and which the Son hath manifested in redeeming them by his blood; for all his full preparation by being a sufficient sacrifice for the sins of all; for all his personal excellencies, and that full and glorious salvation that he hath procured; and for all his free offers of these, and frequent and earnest invitation of sinners; yet many do make light of all this, and prefer their worldly enjoyments before it. The ordinary treatment of all these offers, invitations, and benefits, is by contempt.

Not that all, do so, or that all continue to do so, who were once guilty of it; for God hath his chosen whom he will compel to come in. But till the Spirit of grace overpower the dead and obstinate hearts of men, they hear the gospel as a common story, and the great matters contained in it go not to the heart.

The method in which I shall handle this doctrine is this.

I. I shall shew you what it is that men make light of.

II. What this sin of making light of it is.

III. The cause of the sin.

IV. The use of the doctrine.

The thing that carnal hearers make light of is,

1. The doctrine of the gospel itself, which they hear regardlessly. 2. The benefits offered them therein: which are, 1. Christ himself. 2. The benefits which he giveth.

Concerning Christ himself, the gospel, 1. Declareth his person and nature, and the great things that he hath done and suffered for man; his redeeming him from the wrath of God by his blood, and procuring a grant of salvation with himself. Furthermore, the same gospel maketh an offer of Christ to sinners, that if they will accept him on his easy and reasonable terms, he will he their Saviour, the Physician of their souls, their Husband, and their Head.

2. The benefits that he offereth them are these. 1. That with these blessed relations to him, himself and interest in him, they shall have the pardon of all their sins past, and be saved from

God's wrath, and be set in a sure way of obtaining a pardon for all the sins that they shall commit hereafter, so they do but obey sincerely, and turn not again to the rebellion of their unregeneracy. 2. They shall have the Spirit to become their Guide and Sanctifier, and to dwell in their souls, and help them against their enemies, and conform them more and more to his image, and heal their diseases, and bring them back to God. 3. They shall have right to everlasting glory when this life is ended, and shall be raised up thereto at the last; besides many excellent privileges in the way, in means, preservation, and provision, and the foretaste of what they shall enjoy hereafter: all these benefits the gospel offereth to them that will have Christ on his reasonable terms. The sum of all is in 1 John v. 11, 12, "This is the record, that God hath given us eternal life, and this life is in his Son: he that hath the Son hath life, and he that hath not the Son hath not life."

II

What this sin of the making light of the gospel is.

1. To make light of the gospel is to take no great heed to what is spoken, as if it were not a certain truth, or else were a matter that little concerned them; or as if God had not written these things for them. 2. When the gospel doth not affect men, or go to their hearts; but though they seem to attend to what is said, yet men are not awakened by it from their security, nor doth it work in any measure such holy passion in their souls, as matters of such everlasting consequence should do: this is making light of the gospel of salvation. When we tell men what Christ hath done and suffered for their souls, and it scarce moveth them: we tell them of keen and cutting truths, but nothing will pierce them: we can make them hear, but we cannot make them feel; our words take up in the porch of their ears and fancies, but will not enter into the inward parts; as if we spake to men that had no hearts or feeling: this is a making light of Christ and salvation. Acts xxviii.

26, 27, "Hearing ye shall hear, and shall not understand; seeing ye shall see, and shall not perceive. For the heart of this people is waxed gross, and their ears are dull of hearing, and their eyes have they closed," &c.

3. When men have no high estimation of Christ and salvation, but whatsoever they may say with their tongues, or dreamingly and speculatively believe, yet in their serious and practical thoughts they have a higher estimation of the matters of this world, than they have of Christ, and the salvation that he hath purchased; this is a making light of him. When men account the doctrine of Christ to be but a matter of words and names, as Gallio (Acts xviii. 4), or as Festus (Acts xxv. 19), a superstitious matter about one Jesus who was dead, and Paul saith is alive; or ask the preachers of the gospel, as the Athenians, "What will this babbler say?" Acts xvii. 18: this is contempt of Christ.

4. When men are informed of the truths of the gospel, and on what terms Christ and his benefits may be had, and how it is the will of God that they should believe and accept the offer; and that be commandeth to do it upon pain of damnation; and yet men will not consent, unless they could have Christ on terms of their own: they will not part with their worldly contents, nor lay down their pleasures, and profits, and honour at his feet, as being content to take so much of them only as he will give them back, and as is consistent with his will and interest, but think it is a hard saying, that they must forsake all in resolution for Christ: this is a making light of him and their salvation. When men might have part in him and all his benefits if they would, and they will not, unless they may keep the world too: and are resolved to please their flesh, whatever comes of it; this is a high contempt of Christ and everlasting life. In Matt. xiii. 21; Luke xviii. 23, you may find examples of such as I here describe.

5. When men will promise fair, and profess their willingness to have Christ on his terms, and to forsake all for him, but yet do stick to the world and their sinful courses; and when it comes

to practice, will not be removed by all that Christ hath done and said; this is making light of Christ and salvation, Jer. xlii. 5, compared with xliii. 2.

III

The causes of this sin are the next thing to be inquired after. It may seem a wonder that ever men, that have the use of their reason, should be so sottish as to make light of matters of such consequence. But the cause is,

1. Some men understand not the very sense of the words of the gospel when they hear them; and how can they be taken with that which they understand not? Though we speak to them in plain English, and study to speak it as plain as we can, yet people have so estranged themselves from God, and the matters of their own happiness, that they know not what we say; as if we spoke in another language, and as if they were under that judgment, Isa. xxviii. 11, "With stammering lips, and with another tongue, will he speak to this people."

2. Some that do understand the words that we speak, yet because they are carnal, understand not the matter. "For the natural man receiveth not the things of the Spirit of God, neither can he know them, because they are spiritually discerned," 1 Cor. ii. 14. They are earthly, and these things are heavenly, John iii. 12. These things of the Spirit are not well known by bare hearsay, but by spiritual taste, which none have but those that are taught by the Holy Ghost (1 Cor. ii. 12), that we may know the things that are given us of God.

3. A carnal man apprehendeth not a suitableness in these spiritual and heavenly things to his mind, and therefore he sets light by them, and hath no mind of them. When you tell him of everlasting glory, he heareth you as if you were persuading him to go play with the sun: they are matters of another world, and out of his element; and therefore he hath no more delight in them than

a fish would have to be in the fairest meadow, or than a swine hath in a jewel, or a dog in a piece of gold: they may be good to others, but he cannot apprehend them as suitable to him, because he hath a nature that is otherwise inclined: he savoureth not the things of the Spirit, Rom. viii. 5.

4. The main cause of the slighting of Christ and salvation is, a secret root of unbelief in men's hearts. Whatsoever they may pretend, they do not soundly and thoroughly believe the Word of God: they are taught in general to say the gospel is true; but they never saw the evidence of its truth so far, as thoroughly to persuade them of it; nor have they got their souls settled on the infallibility of God's testimony, nor considered of the truth of the particular doctrines revealed in the Scripture, so far as soundly to believe them. Oh did you all but soundly believe the words of this gospel, of the evil of sin, of the need of Christ, and what he hath done for you, and what you must be and do if ever you will be saved by him; and what will become of you for ever if you do it not; I dare say it would cure the contempt of Christ, and you would not make so light of the matters of your salvation. But men do not believe while they say they do, and would face us down that they do, and verily think that they do themselves. There is a root of bitterness, and an evil heart of unbelief, that make them depart from the living God, Heb. ii. 12; iv. 1, 2, 6. Tell any man in this congregation that he shall have a gift of ten thousand pounds, if he will but go to London for it; if he believe you, he will go; but if he believe not, he will not; and if he will not go, you may be sure he believeth not, supposing that he is able. I know a slight belief may stand with a wicked life; such as men have of the truth of a prognostication, it may be true, and it may be false; but a true and sound belief is not consistent with so great neglect of the things that are believed.

5. Christ and salvation are made light of by the world, because of their desperate hardness of heart. The heart is hard naturally, and by custom in sinning made more hard, especially by long abuse of

mercy, and neglect of the means of grace, and resisting the Spirit of God. Hence it is that men are turned into such stones: and till God cure them of the stone of the heart, no wonder if they feel not what they know, or regard not what we say, but make light of all: it is hard preaching a stone into tears, or making a rock to tremble. You may stand over a dead body long enough, and say to it, O thou carcass, when thou hast lain rotting and mouldered to dust till the resurrection, God will then call thee to account for thy sin, and cast thee into everlasting fire, before you can make it feel what we say, or fear the misery that is never so truly threatened: when men's hearts are like the highway that is trodden to hardness by long custom in sinning, or like the clay that is hardened to a stone by the heat of those mercies that should have melted them into repentance; when they have consciences seared with a hot iron as the apostle speaks (1 Tim. iv. 2), no wonder then if they be past feeling, and working all uncleaness with greediness do make light of Christ and everlasting glory. Oh that this were not the case of too many of our hearers! Had we but *living souls* to speak to, they would hear, and feel, and not make light of what we say. I know they are naturally alive, but they are spiritually dead, as Scripture witnesseth, Eph. ii. 3. Oh if there were one spark of the life of grace in them, the doctrine salvation by Jesus Christ would appear to them to be the weightiest business in the world! Oh how confident should I be, methinks, to prevail with men, and to take them off this world, and bring them to mind the matters of another world, if I spake but to men that had life, and sense, and reason! But when we speak to blocks and dead men, how should we be regarded? Oh how sad a case are these in, that are fallen under this fearful judgment of spiritual madness and deadness! To have a blind mind, and a hard heart, to be sottish and senseless (Mark iv. 12; John xii. 40), lest they should be converted, and their sin should he forgiven them.

6. Christ and salvation are made light of by the world. because they are wholly enslaved to their sense, and taken up with lower

things: the matters of another world are out of sight, and so far from their senses, that they cannot regard them; but present things are nearer them, in their eyes, and in their hands. There must be a living faith to prevail over sense, before men can be so taken with things that are not seen, though they have the Word of God for their security, as to neglect and let go things that are still before their eyes. Sense works with great advantage, and therefore doth much in resisting faith where it is; no wonder then if it carry all before it, where there is no true and lively faith to resist, and to lead the soul to higher things. This cause of making light of Christ and salvation is expressed here in my text: one went to his farm, and another to his merchandise: men have houses and lands to look after; they have wife and children to mind; they have their body and outward estate to regard; therefore they forget that they have a God, a Redeemer, a soul to mind: these matters of the world are still with them. They see these, but they see not God, nor Christ, nor their souls, nor everlasting glory. These things are near at hand, and therefore work naturally, and so work forcibly; but the others are thought on as a great way off, and therefore too distant to work on their affections, or be at the present so much regarded by them. Their body hath life and sense, therefore if they want meat, or drink, or clothes, will feel their want, and tell them of it, and give them no rest till their wants be supplied, and therefore they cannot make light of their bodily necessities; but their souls in spiritual respects are dead, and therefore feel not their wants, but will let them alone in their greatest necessities; and be as quiet when they are starved and languishing to destruction, as if all were well, and nothing ailed them. And hereupon poor people are wholly taken up in providing for the body, as if they had nothing else to mind. They have their trades and callings to follow, and so much to do from morning to night, that they can find no time for matters of salvation: Christ would teach them, but they have no leisure to hear him: the Bible is before them, but they cannot have time to read it; a minister is in the town with them, but they cannot have time to go to enquire of him what they should do to be saved: and when they do hear, their hearts are so full of the world, and carried away with these lower matters, that they cannot mind the things which they hear. They are so full of the thoughts, and desires, and cares of this world, that there is no room to pour into them the water of life. The cares of the world do choke the word, and make it become unfruitful, Matt. xiii. 32. Men cannot serve two masters, God and mammon; but they will lean to the one, and despise the other, Matt. vi. 24. He that loveth the world, the love of the Father is not in him, 1 John ii. 15, 16. Men cannot choose but set light by Christ and salvation, while they set so much by any thing on earth. It is that which is highly esteemed among men that is abominable in the sight of God, Luke xvi. 15. Oh, this is the ruin of many thousand souls! It would grieve the heart of any honest Christian to see how eagerly this vain world is followed every where and how little men set by Christ and the world to come; to compare the care that men have for the world, with the care of their souls: and the time that they lay out on the world, with that time they lay out for their salvation: to see how the world fills their mouths, their hands, their houses, their hearts, and Christ hath little more than a bare title: to come into their company, and hear no discourse but of the world; to come into their houses, and hear and see nothing but for the world, as if this world would last for ever, or would purchase them another. When I ask sometimes the ministers of the gospel how their labours succeed, they tell me, People continue still the same, and give up themselves wholly to the world; so that they mind not what ministers say to them, nor give any full entertainment to the word, and all because of the deluding world: and O that too many ministers themselves did not make light of that Christ whom they preach, being drawn away with the love of this world! In a word, men of a worldly disposition do judge of things according to worldly advantages, therefore Christ is slighted; "He is despised and rejected of men, they hide their faces from him, and esteem him not, as seeing no beauty or comeliness in him, that they should desire him," Isa. liii. 3.

7. Christ and salvation are made light of, because men do not soberly consider of the truth and weight of these necessary things. They suffer not their minds so long to dwell upon them, till they procure a due esteem, and deeply affect their heart; did they believe them and not consider of them, how should they work! Oh when men have reason given them to think and consider of the things that most concern them, and yet they will not use it, this causeth their contempt.

8. Christ and salvation are made light of, because men were never sensible of their sin and misery, and extreme necessity of Christ and his salvation; their eyes were never opened to see themselves as they are; nor their hearts soundly humbled in the sense of their condition: if this were done, they would soon be brought to value a Saviour: a truly broken heart can no more make light of Christ and salvation, than a hungry man of his food, or a sick man of the means that would give him ease; but till then our words cannot have access to their hearts: while sin and misery are made light of, Christ and salvation will be made light of; but when these are perceived an intolerable burden, then nothing will serve the turn but Christ. Till men be truly bumbled, they can venture Christ and salvation for a lust, for a little worldly gain, even for less than nothing: but when God hath illuminated them, and broken their hearts, then they would give a world for a Christ; then they must have Christ or they die; all things then are loss and dung to them in regard of the excellent knowledge of Christ, Phil. iii. 8. When they are once pricked in their hearts for sin and misery, then they cry out, "Men and brethren, what shall we do?" Acts ii. 37. When they are awakened by God's judgments, as the poor jailer, then they cry out, "Sirs, what shall I do to be saved?" Acts xvi. 30. This is the reason why God will bring men so low by humiliation, before he brings them to salvation.

9. Men take occasion to make light of Christ by the commonness of the gospel; because they do hear of it every day, the frequency is an occasion to dull their affections; I say, an occasion, for it is no just cause. Were it a rarity it might take more with them; but now, if they hear a minister preach nothing but these saving truths, they say, We have these every day: they make not light of their bread or drink, their health or life, because they possess them every day; they make not light of the sun because it shineth every day; at least they should not, for the mercy is the greater; but Christ and salvation are made light of because they hear of them often; this is, say they, a good, plain, dry sermon. Pearls are trod into the dirt where they are common: they loathe this dry manna: "The full soul loathes the honey-comb; but to the hungry every bitter thing is sweet." Prov. xxvii. 7.

10. Christ and salvation are made light of, because of this disjunctive presumption; either that he is sure enough theirs already, and God that is so merciful, and Christ that hath suffered so much for them, is surely resolved to save them; or else it may easily be obtained at any time, if it be not yet so. A conceited facility to have a part in Christ and salvation at any time doth occasion men to make light of them. It is true, that grace is free, and the offer is universal, according to the extent of the preaching of the gospel; and it is true, that men may have Christ when they will; that is, when they are willing to have him on his terms; but he that hath promised thee Christ if thou be willing, hath not promised to make thee willing: and if thou art not willing now, how canst thou think thou shalt be willing hereafter? If thou canst make thine own heart willing, why is it not done now? Can you do it better when sin hath more hardened it, and God may have given thee over to thyself? O sinners! you might do much, though you are not able of yourselves to come in, if you would now subject yourselves to the working of the Spirit, and set in while the gales of grace continue. But did you know what a hard and impossible thing it is to be so much as willing to have

Christ and grace, when the heart is given over to itself, and the Spirit hath withdrawn its former invitations, you would not be so confident of your own strength to believe and repent; nor would you make light of Christ upon such foolish confidence. If indeed it be so easy a matter as you imagine, for a sinner to believe and repent at any time, how comes it to pass that it is done by so few; but most of the world do perish in their impenitency when they have all the helps and means that we can afford them? It is true, the thing is very reasonable and easy in itself to a pure nature; but while man is blind and dead, these things are in a sort impossible to him, which are never so easy to others. It is the easiest and sweetest life in the world to a gracious soul to live in the love of God, and the delightful thoughts of the life to come, where all their hope and happiness lieth: but to a worldly, carnal heart, it is as easy to remove a mountain as to bring them to this. However, these men are their own condemners; for if they think it so easy a matter to repent and believe, and so to have Christ, and right to salvation, then have they no excuse for neglecting this which they thought so easy. O wretched, impenitent soul! what mean you to say when God shall ask you, Why did you not repent and love your Redeemer above the world, when you thought it so easy that you could do it at any time?

IV

Use 1. We come now to the application: and hence you may be informed of the blindness and folly of all carnal men. How contemptible are their judgments that think Christ and salvation contemptible! And how little reason there is why any should be moved by them, or discouraged by any of their scorns or contradictions!

How shall we sooner know a man to be a fool, than if he know no difference between dung and gold? Is there such a thing as madness in the world, if that man be not mad that sets light by

Christ, and his own salvation, while he daily toils for the dung of the earth? And yet what pity is it to see that a company of poor, ignorant souls will be ashamed of godliness, if such men as these do but deride them! or will think hardly of a holy life, if such as these do speak against it! Hearers, if you see any set light by Christ and salvation, do you set light by that man's wit, and by his words, and hear the reproaches of a holy life as you would hear the words of a madman, not with regard, but with a compassion of his misery.

Use 2. What wonder if we and our preaching be despised, and the best ministers complain of ill success, when the ministry of the apostles themselves did succeed no better? What wonder if, for all that we can say or do, our hearers still set light by Christ and their own salvation, when the apostles' hearers did the same? They that did second their doctrine by miracles, if any men could have shaken and torn in pieces the hearts of sinners, they could have done it; if any could have laid them at their feet, and made them all cry out as some, 'What shall we do?' it would have been they. You may see then that it is not merely for want of good preachers that men make light of Christ and salvation. The first news of such a thing as the pardon of sin, and the hopes of glory, and the danger of everlasting misery, would turn the hearts of men within them, if they were as tractable in spiritual matters as in temporal: but, alas, it is far otherwise. It must not seem any strange thing, nor must it too much discourage the preachers of the gospel, if when they have said all that they can devise to say, to win the hearts of men to Christ, the most do still slight him; and while they bow the knee to him, and honour him with their lips, do yet set so light by him in their hearts, as to prefer every fleshly pleasure or commodity before him. It will be thus with many: let us be glad that it is not thus with all.

Use 3. But for closer application, seeing this is the great condemning sin, before we inquire after it into the hearts of our hearers, it beseems us to begin at home, and see that we, who are preachers of the gospel, be not guilty of it ourselves. The Lord forbid that they that have undertaken the sacred office of revealing the excellencies of Christ to the world, should make light of him themselves, and slight that salvation which they do daily preach. The Lord knows we are all of us so low in our estimation of Christ, and do this great work so negligently, that we have cause to be ashamed of our best sermons; but should this sin prevail in us, we were the most miserable of all men. Brethren, I love not censoriousness; yet dare not befriend so vile a sin in myself or others, under pretence of avoiding it: especially when there is so great necessity that it should be healed first in them that make it their work to heal it in others. Oh that there were no cause to complain that Christ and salvation are made light of by the preachers of it! But, 1. Do not the negligent studies of some speak it out? 2. Doth not their dead and drowsy preaching declare it? Do not they make light of the doctrine they preach, that do it as if they were half asleep, and feel not what they speak themselves?

3. Doth not the carelessness of some men's private endeavours discover it? What do they for souls? how slightly do they reprove sin! How little do they when they are out of the pulpit for the saving of men's souls!

4. Doth not the continued neglect of those things wherein the interest of Christ consisteth discover it? 1. The church's purity and reformation. 2. Its unity.

5. Do not the covetous and worldly lives of too many discover it, losing advantages for men's souls for a little gain to themselves? And most of this is because men are preachers before they are Christians, and tell men of that which they never felt themselves. Of all men on earth there are few that are in so sad a condition as such ministers: and if, indeed, they do believe that Scripture which they preach, methinks it should be terrible to them in their studying and preaching it.

Use 4. Beloved hearers, the office that God hath called us to, is by declaring the glory of his grace, to help under Christ to the saving of men's souls. I hope you think not that I come hither today on any other errand. The Lord knows I had not set a foot out of doors but in hope to succeed in this work for your souls. I have considered, and often considered, what is the matter that so many thousands should perish when God hath done so much for their salvation; and I find this that is mentioned in my text is the cause. It is one of the wonders of the world, that when God hath so loved the world as to send his Son, and Christ hath made a satisfaction by his death sufficient for them all, and offereth the benefits of it so freely to them, even without money or price, that yet the most of the world should perish; yea, the most of those that are thus called by his word! Why, here is the reason, when Christ hath done all this, men make light of it. God hath shewed that he is not unwilling; and Christ hath shewed that he is not unwilling that men should be restored to God's favour and be saved; but men are actually unwilling themselves. God takes not pleasure in the death of sinners, but rather that they return and live, Ezek. xxxiii. 11. But men take such pleasure in sin, that they will die before they will return. The Lord Jesus was content to be their Physician, and hath provided them a sufficient plaster of his own blood: but if men make light of it, and will not apply it, what wonder if they perish alter all? This Scripture giveth us the reason of their perdition. This, sad experience tells us, the most of the world is guilty of. It is a most lamentable thing to see how most men do spend their care, their time, their pains, for known vanities, while God and glory are cast aside; that he who is all should seem to them as nothing, and that which is nothing should seem to them as good as all; that God should set mankind in such a race where heaven or hell is their certain end, and that they should sit down, and loiter, or run after the childish toys of the world, and so much forget the prize that they should run for. Were it but possible for one of us to see the whole of this business as the all-seeing God doth; to see at one view both heaven and hell, which men are so near; and see what most men in the world are minding, and what they are doing every day, it would be the saddest sight that could be imagined. Oh how should we marvel at their madness, and lament their self-delusion! Oh poor distracted world! what is it you run after? and what is it that you neglect? If God had never told them what they were sent into the world to do, or whither they were going, or what was before them in another world, then they had been excusable; but he hath told them over and over, till they were weary of it. Had he left it doubtful, there had been some excuse; but it is his sealed word, and they profess to believe it, and would take it ill of us if we should question whether they do believe it or not.

Beloved, I come not to accuse any of you particularly of this crime; but seeing it is the commonest cause of men's destruction, I suppose you will judge it the fittest matter for our inquiry, and deserving our greatest care for the cure. To which end I shall, 1. Endeavour the conviction of the guilty. 2. Shall give them such considerations as may tend to humble and reform them. 3. I shall conclude with such direction as may help them that are willing to escape the destroying power of this sin. And. for the first, consider,

I

It is the case of most sinners to think themselves freest from those sins that they are most enslaved to; and one reason why we cannot reform them, is because we cannot convince them of their guilt. It is the nature of sin so far to blind and befool the sinner, that he knoweth not what he doth, but thinketh he is free from it when it reigneth in him, or when he is committing it: it bringeth men to be so much unacquainted with themselves, that they know not what they think, or what they mean and intend, nor what they love or hate, much less what they are habituated and disposed to. They are alive to sin, and dead to all the reason, consideration, and resolution that should recover them, as if it were only by their sinning that we must know they are alive. May I hope that you that hear me to-day are but willing to know the truth of your case, and then I shall be encouraged to proceed to an inquiry. God will judge impartially; why should not we do so? Let me, therefore, by these following questions, try whether none of you are slighters of Christ and your own salvation. And follow me, I beseech you, by putting them close to your own hearts, and faithfully answering them.

1. Things that men highly value will be remembered, they will be matter of their freest and sweetest thoughts. This is a known case.

Do not those then make light of Christ and salvation that think of them so seldom and coldly in comparison of other things? Follow thy own heart, man, and observe what it daily runneth after; and then judge whether it make not light of Christ.

We cannot persuade men to one hour's sober consideration what they should do for an interest in Christ, or in thankfulness for his love, and yet they will not believe that they make light of him.

2. Things that we highly value will be matter of our discourse; the judgment and heart will command the tongue. Freely and delightfully will our speech run after them. This also is a known case.

Do not those then make light of Christ and salvation, that shun the mention of his name, unless it be in a vain or sinful use? Those that love not the company where Christ and salvation is much talked of, but think it troublesome, precise discourse: that had rather hear some merry jests, or idle tales, or talk of their riches or business in the world. When you may follow them from morning to night, and scarce have a savoury word of Christ; but perhaps some slight and weary mention of him sometimes; judge whether these make not light of Christ and salvation. How seriously do they talk of the world (Psal. cxliv. 8, 11) and speak vanity! but how heartlessly do they make mention of Christ and salvation!

3. The things that we highly value we would secure the possession of, and therefore would take any convenient course to have all doubts and fears about them well resolved. Do not those men

then make light of Christ and salvation that have lived twenty or thirty years in uncertainty whether they have any part in these or not, and yet never seek out for the right resolution of their doubts? Are all that hear me this day certain they shall be saved? Oh that they were! Oh, had you not made light of salvation, you could not so easily bear such doubtings of it; you could not rest till you had made it sure, or done your best to make it sure. Have you nobody, to inquire of, that might help you in such a work? Why, you have ministers that are purposely appointed to that office. Have you gone to them, and told them the doubtfulness of your case, and asked their help in the judging of your condition? Alas, ministers may sit in their studies from one year to another, before ten persons among a thousand will come to them on such an errand! Do not these make light of Christ and salvation? When the gospel pierceth the heart indeed, they cry out, "Men and brethren, what shall we do to be saved?" Acts xvi. 30. Trembling and astonished, Paul cries out, "Lord, what wilt thou have me to do?" Acts ix. 6. And so did the convinced Jews to Peter, Acts ii. 37. But when hear we such questions?

4. The things that we value do deeply affect us, and some motions will be in the heart according to our estimation of them. O sirs, if men made not light of these things, what working would there be in the hearts of all our hearers! What strange affections would it raise in them to hear of the matters of the world to come! How would their hearts melt before the power of the gospel! What sorrow would be wrought in the discovery of their sins! What astonishment at the consideration of their misery! What unspeakable joy at the glad tidings of salvation by the blood of Christ! What resolution would be raised in them upon the discovery of their duty! Oh what hearers should we have, if it were not for this sin! Whereas now we are liker to weary them, or preach them asleep with matters of this unspeakable moment. We talk to them of Christ and salvation till we make their heads ache: little would one think by their careless carriage

that they heard and regarded what we said, or thought we spoke at all to them.

5. Our estimation of things will be seen in the diligence of our endeavours. That which we highliest value, we shall think no pains too great to obtain. Do not those men then make light of Christ and salvation, that think all too much that they do for them; that murmur at his service, and think it too grievous for them to endure? that ask of his service as Judas of the ointment, What need this waste? Cannot men be saved without so much ado? This is more ado than needs. For the world they will labour all the day, and all their lives; but for Christ and salvation they are afraid of doing too much. Let us preach to them as long as we will, we cannot bring them to relish or resolve upon a life of holiness. Follow them to their houses, and you shall not hear them read a chapter, nor call upon God with their families once a day: nor will they allow him that one day in seven which he hath separated to his service. But pleasure, or worldly business, or idleness, must have a part. And many of them are so far hardened as to reproach them that will not be as mad as themselves. And is not Christ worth the seeking? Is not everlasting salvation worth more than all this? Doth not that soul make light of all these, that thinks his ease more worth than they? Let but common sense judge.

6. That which we most highly value, we think we cannot buy too dear: Christ and salvation are freely given, and yet the most of men go without them, because they cannot enjoy the world and them together. They are called but to part with that which would hinder them from Christ, and they will not do it. They are called but to give God his own, and to resign all to his will, and let go the profits and pleasures of this world, when they must let go either Christ or them, and they will not. They think this too dear a bargain, and say they cannot spare these things: they must hold their credit with men; they must look to their estates: how shall they live else? They must have their pleasure, whatsoever becomes of Christ and salvation: as if they could live without

Christ better than without these: as if they were afraid of being losers by Christ, or could make a saving match by losing their souls to gain the world. Christ hath told us over and over, that if we will not forsake all for him we cannot be his disciples, Matt. x. Far are these men from forsaking all, and yet will needs think that they are his disciples indeed.

7. That which men highly esteem, they would help their friends to as well as themselves. Do not those men make light of Christ and salvation, that can take so much care to leave their children portions in the world, and do so little to help them to heaven? that provide outward necessaries so carefully for their families, but do so little to the saving of their souls? Their neglected children and friends will witness, that either Christ, or their children's souls, or both, were made light of.

8. That which men highly esteem, they will so diligently seek after, that you may see it in the success, if it be a matter within their reach. You may see how many make light of Christ, by the little knowledge they have of him, and the little communion with him, and communication from him; and the little, yea, none of his special grace in them. Alas! how many ministers can speak it to the sorrow of their hearts, that many of their people know almost nothing of Christ, though they hear of him daily! Nor know they what they must do to be saved: if we ask them an account of these things, they answer as if they understood not what we say to them, and tell us they are no scholars, and therefore think they are excusable for their ignorance. Oh if these men had not made light of Christ and their salvation, but had bestowed but half as much pains to know and enjoy him as they have done to understand the matters of their trades and callings in the world, they would not have been so ignorant as they are: they make light of these things, and therefore will not be at the pains to study or learn them. When men that can learn the hardest trade in a few years, have not learned a catechism, nor how to understand their creed, under twenty or thirty years' preaching, nor can abide to

be questioned about such things; doth not this shew that they have slighted them in their hearts? How will these despisers of Christ and salvation be able one day to look him in the face, and to give an account of these neglects?

2

Thus much I have spoken in order to your conviction. Do not some of your consciences by this time smite you, and say, I am the man that have made light of my salvation? If they do not, it is because you make light of it still, for all that is said to you. But because, if it be the will of the Lord, I would fain have this damning distemper cured, and am loth to leave you in such a desperate condition, if I knew how to remedy it, I will give you some considerations, which may move you, if you be men of reason and understanding, to look better about you; and I beseech you to weigh them, and make use of them as we go, and lay open our hearts to the work of grace, and sadly bethink you what a case you are in, if you prove such as make light of Christ.

Consider, 1. Thou makest light of him that made not light of thee who didst deserve it. Thou wast worthy of nothing but contempt. As a man, what art thou but a worm to God? As a sinner, thou art far viler than a toad: yet Christ was so far from making light of thee and thy happiness, that he came down into the flesh, and lived a life of suffering, and offered himself a sacrifice to the justice which thou hadst provoked, that thy miserable soul might have a remedy. It is no less than miracles of love and mercy, that he hath shewed to us: and yet shall we slight them after all?

Angels admire them, whom they less concern (1 Pet. i. 12), and shall redeemed sinners make light of them? What barbarous, yea, devilish, yea, worse than devilish ingratitude is this! The devils never had a saviour offered them, but thou hast, and dost thou yet make light of Him?

2. Consider, the work of man's salvation by Jesus Christ is the master-piece of all the works of God, wherein he would have

his love and mercy to be magnified. As the creation declareth his goodness and power, so doth redemption his goodness and mercy; he hath contrived the very frame of his worship so, that it shall much consist in the magnifying of this work; and after all this, will you make light of it? "His name is Wonderful," Isa. ix. 6. "He did the work that none could do," John xv. 24. "Greater love could none shew than his," John xv. 13. How great was the evil and misery that he delivered us from! the good procured for us! All are wonders, from his birth to his ascension; from our new birth to our glorification, all are wonders of matchless mercy—and yet do you make light of them?

3. You make light of matters of greatest excellency and moment in the world: you know not what it is that you slight: had you well known, you could not have done it. As Christ said to the woman of Samaria (John iv. 10), Hadst thou known who it is that speakest to thee, thou wouldst have asked of him the waters of life: had they known they would not have crucified the Lord of glory, 1 Cor. ii. 8. So had you known what Christ is, you would not have made light of him; had you been one day in heaven, and but seen what they possess, and seen also what miserable souls must endure that are shut out, you would never sure have made so light of Christ again.

O sirs, it is no trifles or jesting matters that the gospel speaks of. I must needs profess to you, that when I have the most serious thoughts of these things myself, I am ready to marvel that such amazing matters do not overwhelm the souls of men; that the greatness of the subject doth not so overmatch our understandings and affections, as even to drive men beside themselves, but that God hath always somewhat allayed it by the distance: much more that men should be so blockish as to make light of them. O Lord, that men did but know what everlasting glory and everlasting torments are; would they then bear us as they do? would they read and think of these things as they do? I profess I have been ready to wonder, when I have heard such weighty things delivered, how people can forbear crying out in the congregation; much more how they can rest till they have gone to their ministers, and learned what they should do to be saved, that this great business might be put out of doubt. Oh that heaven and hell should work no more on men! Oh that everlastingness should work no more! Oh how can you forbear when you are alone to think with yourselves what it is to be everlastingly in joy or in torment! I wonder that such thoughts do not break your sleep; and that they come not in your mind when you are about your labour! I wonder how you can almost do any thing else! how you can have any quietness in your minds! how you can eat, or drink, or rest, till you have got some ground of everlasting consolations! Is that a man or a corpse that is not affected with matters of this moment? that can be readier to sleep than to tremble when he heareth how be must stand at the bar of God? Is that a man or a clod of clay that can rise and lie down without being deeply affected with his everlasting estate? that can follow his worldly business, and make nothing of the great business of salvation or damnation; and that when they know it is hard at hand! Truly, sirs, when I think of the weight of the matter, I wonder at the very best of God's saints upon earth that they are no better, and do no more in so weighty a case. I wonder at those whom the world accounteth more holy than needs, and scorns for making too much ado, that they can put off Christ and their souls with so little; that they pour not out their souls in every supplication; that they are not more taken up with God; that their thoughts be not more serious in preparation for their account. I wonder that they be not a hundred times more strict in their lives, and more laborious and unwearied in striving for the crown, than they are. And for myself, as I am ashamed of my dull and careless heart, and of my slow and unprofitable, course of life; so the Lord knows I am ashamed of every sermon that I preach: when I think what I have been speaking of, and who sent me, and what men's salvation or damnation is so much concerned in it, I am ready to tremble, lest God should judge me as a slighter of his truth, and the souls of men, and lest in the best sermon I should be guilty of their blood. Methinks we should not speak a word to men in matters of such consequence without tears, or the greatest earnestness that possibly we can: were not we too much guilty of the sin which we reprove, it would be so. Whether we are alone, or in company, methinks our end, and such an end, should still be in our mind, and as before our eyes; and we should sooner forget any thing, and set light by any thing, or by all things, than by this.

Consider, 4. Who is it that sends this weighty message to you? Is it not God himself? Shall the God of heaven speak, and men make light of it? You would not slight the voice of an angel, or a prince.

5. Whose salvation is it that you make light of? Is it not your own? Are you no more near or dear to yourselves than to make light of your own happiness or misery? Why, sirs, do you not care whether you be saved or damned? is self-love lost? are you turned your own enemies? As he that slighteth his meat doth slight his life; so if you slight Christ, whatsoever you may think, you will find it was your own salvation that you slighted. Hear what he saith, "All they that hate me love death," Prov. viii. 36.

6. Your sin is greater, in that you profess to believe the gospel which you make so light of. For a professed infidel to do it that believes not that ever Christ died, or rose again; or doth not believe that there is a heaven or hell; this were no such marvel: but for you that make it your creed, and your very religion, and call yourselves Christians, and have been baptized into this faith, and seemed to stand to it, this is the wonder, and hath no excuse. What! believe that you shall live in endless joy or torment, and yet make no more of it to escape torment, and obtain that joy! What! believe that God will shortly judge you, and yet make no more preparation for it! Either say plainly, I am no Christian, I do not believe these wonderful things, I will believe nothing but what I see; or else let your hearts be affected with your belief, and live

as you say you do believe. What do you think when you repeat the creed, and mention Christ's judgment and everlasting life?

7. What are these things you set so much by, as to prefer them before Christ and the saving of your souls? Have you found a better friend, a greater and surer happiness than this? Good Lord! what dung is it that men make so much of, while they set so light by everlasting glory! What toys are they that they are daily taken up with, while matters of life and death are neglected! Why, sirs, if you had every one a kingdom in your hopes, what were it in comparison of the everlasting kingdom? I cannot but look upon all the glory and dignity of this world, lands and lordships, crowns and kingdoms, even as on some brain-sick, beggarly fellow, that borroweth fine clothes, and plays the part of a king or a lord for an hour on a stage, and then comes down, and the sport is ended, and they are beggars again. Were it not for God's interest in the authority of magistrates, or for the service they might do him, I should judge no better of them. For as to their own glory, it is but a smoke: what matter is it whether you live poor or rich, unless it were a greater matter to die rich than it is? You know well enough that death levels all. What matter is it at judgment, whether you be to answer for the life of a rich man or a poor man? Is Dives then any better than Lazarus? O that men knew what a poor deceiving shadow they grasp at, while they let go the everlasting substance! The strongest. and richest, and most voluptuous sinners, do but lay in fuel for their sorrows, while they think they are gathering together a treasure. Alas! they are asleep, and dream that they are happy; but when they awake, what a change will they find! Their crown is made of thorns: their pleasure hath such a sting as will stick in the heart through all eternity, except unfeigned repentance do prevent it. O how sadly will these wretches be convinced, ere long, what a foolish bargain they made in selling Christ and their salvation for these trifles! Let your farms and merchandise then save you if they can; and do that for you that Christ would have done. Cry

then to thy Baal to save thee! Oh what thoughts have drunkards and adulterers, &c. Of Christ, that will not part with the basest lust for him! "For a piece of bread," saith Solomon, "such men do transgress," Prov. xxviii. 11.

8. To set so light by Christ and salvation, is a certain mark that thou hast no part in them, and if thou so continue, that Christ will set as light by thee: "Those that honour him he will honour, and those that despise him shall be lightly esteemed," 1 Sam. ii. 30. Thou wilt feel one day that thou canst not live without him; thou wilt confess then thy need of him; and then thou mayest go look for a saviour where thou wilt; for he will be no saviour for thee hereafter, that wouldst not value him, and submit to him here. Then who will prove the loser by thy contempt? O what a thing will it be for a poor miserable soul to cry to Christ for help in the day of extremity, and to hear so sad an answer as this! Thou didst set light by me and my law in the day of thy prosperity, and I will now set as light by thee in thy adversity. Read Prov. i. 24, to the end. Thou that, as Esau, didst sell thy birthright for a mess of pottage, shalt then find no place for repentance, though thou seek it with tears, Heb. xii. 17. Do you think that Christ shed his blood to save them that continue to make light of it? and to save them that value a cup of drink or a lust before his salvation? I tell you, sirs, though you set so light by Christ and salvation, God doth not so: he will not give them on such terms as these: he valueth the blood of his Son, and the everlasting glory; and he will make you value them if ever you have them. Nay, this will be thy condemnation, and leaveth no remedy. All the world cannot save him that sets light by Christ, Heb. ii. 3; Luke xiv. 24. None of them shall taste of his supper, Matt. x. 37. Nor can you blame him to deny you what you made light of yourselves. Can you find fault if you miss of the salvation which you slighted?

9. The time is near when Christ and salvation will not be made light of as now they are. When God hath shaken those careless souls out of their bodies, and you must answer for all your sins

in your own name; oh then what would you give for a saviour! When a thousand bills shall be brought in against you, and none to relieve you then you will consider, Oh! Christ would now have stood between me and the wrath of God: had I not despised him, he would have answered all. When you see the world hath left you, and your companions in sin have deceived themselves and you, and all your merry days are gone; then what would you give for that Christ and salvation that now you account not worth your labour! Do you think when you see the judgment set, and you are doomed to everlasting perdition for your wickedness, that you should then make as light of Christ as now? Why will you not judge now as you know you shall judge then? Will he then be worth ten thousand worlds? and is he not now worth your highest estimation and dearest affection?

10. God will not only deny thee that salvation thou madest light of, but he will take from thee all that which thou didst value before it: he that most highly esteems Christ shall have him, and the creatures so far as they are good here, and him without the creature hereafter, because the creature is not useful; and he that sets more by the creature than by Christ, shall have some of the creature without Christ here, and neither Christ nor it hereafter.

So much of these considerations, which may shew the true face of this heinous sin.

What think you now, friends, of this business? Do you not see by this time what a case that soul is in that maketh light of Christ and salvation? What need then is there that you should take heed lest this should prove your own case! The Lord knows it is too common a case. Whoever is found guilty at the last of this sin, it were better for that man he had never been born. It were better for him he had been a Turk [Muslim] or Indian [Hindu], that never had heard the name of a Saviour, and that never had salvation offered to him: for such men "have no cloak for their sin," John xv. 22. Besides all the rest of their sins, they have this killing sin to answer for, which will undo them. And this will aggravate their misery, that Christ whom they set light by must be their Judge, and for this sin will he judge them. Oh that such would now consider how they will answer that question that Christ put to their predecessors, "How will ye escape the damnation of hell?" Matt. xxiii. 33: or, "how shall we escape if we neglect so great salvation?" Heb. ii. 3. Can you escape without a Christ? or will a despised Christ save you then? If he be accursed that sets light by father or mother (Deut. xxvii. 16), what then is he that sets light by Christ? It was the heinous sin of the Jews, that among them were found such as set light by father and mother, Ezek. xxii. 7. But among us, men slight the Father of spirits! In the name of God, brethren, I beseech you to consider how you will then bear his anger which you now make light of! You that cannot make light of a little sickness or want, or of natural death, no, not of a tooth-ache, but groan as if you were undone; how will you then make light of the fury of the Lord, which will burn against the contemners of his grace! Doth it not behove you beforehand to think of these things?

3

Hitherto I have been convincing you of the evil of the sin, and the danger that followeth: I come now to know your resolution for the time to come. What say you? Do you mean to set as light by Christ and salvation as hitherto you have done; and to be the same men after all this? I hope not. Oh let not your ministers that would fain save you, be brought in as witnesses against you to condemn you; at least, I beseech you, put not this upon me. Why, sirs, if the Lord shall say to us at judgment, Did you never tell these men what Christ did for their souls, and what need they had of him, and how nearly it did concern them to look to their salvation, that they made light of it? We must needs say the truth; Yea, Lord, we told them of it as plainly as we could; we would have gone on our knees to them if we had thought it would have prevailed; we did entreat them as earnestly as we could to consider these things: they heard of these things every day; but, alas, we could never get them to their hearts: they gave us the hearing, but they made light of all that we could say to them. Oh! sad will it prove on your side, if you force us to such an answer as this.

But if the Lord do move the hearts of any of you, and you resolve to make light of Christ no more; or if any of you say, We do not make light of him; let me tell you here in the conclusion what you must do, or else you shall be judged as slighters of Christ and salvation.

And first I will tell you what will not serve the turn.

1. You may have a notional knowledge of Christ, and the necessity of his blood, and of the excellency of salvation, and yet perish as neglecters of him. This is too common among professed Christians. You may say all that other men do of him: what gospel passages had Balaam! Jesus I know, and Paul I know, the very devils could say, who believe and tremble, James ii. 19.

2. You may weep at the history of Christ's passion, when you read how he was used by the Jews, and yet make light of him, and perish for so doing.

3. You may come desirously to his word and ordinances. Herod heard gladly; so do many that yet must perish as neglecters of salvation.

4. You may in a fit of fear have strong desires after a Christ, to ease you, and to save you from God's wrath, as Saul had of David to play before him; and yet you may perish for making light of Christ.

5. You may obey him in many things so far as will not ruin you in the world, and escape much of the pollutions of the world by his knowledge, and yet neglect him.

6. You may suffer and lose much for him, so far as leaveth you an earthly felicity; as Ananias; and the young man, Matt. xix. 16–22. Some parcels of their pleasures and profits many will

part with in hope of salvation, that shall perish everlastingly for valuing it no more.

7. You may be esteemed by others a man zealous for Christ, and loved and admired upon that account, and yet be one that shall perish for making light of him.

8. You may verily think yourselves, that you set more by Christ and salvation than any thing, and yet be mistaken, and be judged as contemners of him: Christ justifieth not all that justify themselves.

9. You may be zealous preachers of Christ and salvation, and reprove others for this neglect, and lament the sin of the world in the like expression as I have done this day; and yet if you or I have no better evidence to prove our hearty esteem of Christ and salvation, we are undone for all this.

4

You hear, brethren, what will not serve the turn; will you now hear what persons you must be if you would not be condemned as slighters of Christ? O search whether it be thus with your souls or no!

1. Your esteem of Christ and salvation must be greater than your esteem of all the honours, profits, or pleasures of this world, or else you slight him: no less will be accounted sincere, nor accepted to your salvation. Think not this hard, when there is no comparison in the matters esteemed. To esteem the greatest glory on earth before Christ and everlasting glory, is a greater folly and wrong to Christ, than to esteem a dog before your prince, would be folly in you, and a wrong to him. Scripture is plain in this; "He that loveth father or mother, wife, children, house, land, or his own life, more than me, is not worthy of me, and cannot be my disciple," Matt. x. 37; Luke xiv. 26.

2. You must manifest this esteem of Christ and salvation in your daily endeavours and seeking after him, and in parting with any thing that he shall require of you. God is a Spirit, and will not take a hypocritical profession instead of the heart and spiritual service

which he commandeth. He will have the heart or nothing; and the chief room in the heart too: these must be had.

If you say that you do not make light of Christ, or will not hereafter; let me try you in these few particulars, whether indeed you mean as you say, and do not dissemble.

1. Will you for the time to come make Christ and salvation the chiefest matter of your care and study? Thrust them not out of your thoughts as a needless or unprofitable subject; nor allow it only some running, slight thoughts, which will not affect you. But will you make it your business once a day to bethink you soberly, when you are alone, what Christ hath done for you, and what he will do, if you do not make light of it; and what it is to be everlastingly happy or miserable? And what all things in this world are in comparison of your salvation; and how they will shortly leave you; and what mind you will be then of, and how will esteem them? Will you promise me now and then to make it your business to withdraw yourselves from the world, and set yourselves to such considerations as these? If you will not, are not you slighters of Christ and salvation, that will not be persuaded soberly to think on them? This is my first question to put you to the trial, whether you will value Christ or not.

2. Will you for the time to come set more by the Word of God, which contains the discovery of these excellent things, and is your charter for salvation, and your guide thereunto? You cannot set by Christ, but you must set by his word: therefore the despisers of it are threatened with destruction, Prov. xiii. 13. Will you therefore attend to the public preaching of this Word; will you read it daily; will you resolve to obey it whatever it may cost you? if you will not do this, but make light of the Word of God, you shall be judged as such as make light of Christ and salvation, whatever you may fondly promise to yourselves.

3. Will you for the time to come esteem more of the officers of Christ, whom he hath purposely appointed to guide you to salvation; and will you make use of them for that end? Alas, it

is not to give the minister a good word, and speak well of him, and pay him his tithes duly, that will serve the turn: it is for the necessity of your souls that God hath set them in his church; that they may be as physicians under Christ, or his apothecaries to apply his remedies to your spiritual diseases, not only in public, but also in private: that you may have some to go to for the resolving of your doubts, and for your instruction where you are ignorant, and for the help of their exhortations and prayers. Will you use hereafter to go to your ministers privately, and solicit them for advice? And if you have not such of your own as are fit, get advice from others; and ask them, What you shall do to be saved? how to prepare for death and judgement? And will you obey the Word of God in their mouths? If you will not do this much, nor so much as inquire of those that should teach you, nor use the means which Christ hath established in his church for your help, your own consciences shall one day witness that you were such as made light of Christ and salvation. If any of you doubt whether it be your duty thus to ask counsel of your teachers, as sick men do of their physicians, let your own necessities resolve you, let God's express Word resolve you; see what is said of the priests of the Lord, even before Christ's coming, when much of their work did lie in ceremonials: "My covenant was with him of life and peace: and I gave them to him (to Levi) for the fear wherewith he feared me, and was afraid before my name. The law of truth was in his mouth, and iniquity was not found in his lips; he walked with me in peace and equity, and did turn many away from iniquity. For the priest's lips should keep knowledge, and they should seek the law at his mouth: for he is the messenger of the Lord of hosts," Mal. ii. 5–7.

Nay, you must not only inquire, and submit to their advice, but also to their just reprehensions, and church censures; and without proud repining submit to the discipline of Christ in their hands, if it shall be used in the congregations whereof you are members.

4. Will you for the time to come make conscience of daily and

earnest prayer to God, that you may have a part in Christ and salvation? Do not go out of doors till you have breathed out these desires to God; do not lie down to rest till you have breathed out these desires: say not, God knoweth my necessity without so often praying; for though he do, yet he will have you to know them, and feel them, and exercise your desires and all the graces of his Spirit in these duties: it is he that hath commanded to pray continually, though he know your needs without it, 1 Thess. v. 17. Christ himself spent whole nights in prayer, and encourageth us to this course, Luke xviii. 1. If you will not be persuaded to this much, how can you say that you make not light of Christ and salvation?

5. Will you for the time to come resolvedly cast away your known sins at the command of Christ? If you have been proud, or contentious, or malicious, and revengeful, be so no more. If you have been adulterers, or swearers, or cursers, be so no more. You cannot hold these, and yet set by Christ and salvation.

What say you? Are you resolved to let them go? If not, when you know it is the will of Christ, and he hath told you such shall not enter into his kingdom, do not you make light of him?

6. Will you for the time to come serve God in the dearest as well as in the cheapest part of his service? not only with your tongues, but with your purses and your deeds? Shall the poor find that you set more by Christ than this world? Shall it appear in any good uses that God calls you to be liberal in, according to your abilities? "Pure religion and undefiled before God is this, to visit the fatherless and the widows in their affliction." James i. 27. Will you resolve to stick to Christ, and make sure this work of salvation, though it cost you all that you have in the world? If you think these terms too dear, you make light of Christ, and will be judged accordingly.

7. Will you for the time to come make much of all things that tend to your salvation; and take every help that God offereth you, and gladly make use of all his ordinances? Attend upon his strengthening sacraments; spend the Lord's own day in these

holy employments; instruct your children and servants in these things, Deut. vi. 6, 7; get into good company that set their faces heavenward, and will teach you the way, and help you thither; and take heed of the company of wicked scorners, or foolish, voluptuous, fleshly men, or any that would hinder you in this work. Will you do these things? Or will you shew that you are slighters of Christ by neglecting them?

8. Will you do all this with delight; not as your toil, but as your pleasure? And take it for your highest honour that you may be Christ's disciples, and may be admitted to serve and worship him; and rejoice with holy confidence in the sufficiency of that sacrifice by which you may have pardon of all your failings, and right to the inheritance of the saints in light? If you will do these things sincerely, you will shew that you set by Christ and salvation; else not.

Dearly beloved in the Lord, I have now done that work which I came upon; what effect it hath, or will have, upon your hearts, I know not, nor is it any further in my power to accomplish that which my soul desireth for you. Were it the Lord's will that I might have my wish herein, the words that you have this day heard should so stick by you, that the secure should be awakened by them, and none of you should perish by the slighting of your salvation. I cannot now follow you to your several habitations to apply this word to your particular necessities; but O that I could make every man's conscience a preacher to himself that it might do it, which is ever with you!—That the next time you go prayerless to bed, or about your business, conscience might cry out, Dost thou set no more by Christ and thy salvation? That the next time you are tempted to think hardly of a holy and diligent life (I will not say to deride it as more ado than needs), conscience might cry out to thee, Dost thou set so light by Christ and thy salvation? That the next time you are ready to rush upon known sin, and to please your fleshly desires against the command of God, conscience might cry out, Is Christ and salvation no more worth, than to cast them away, or venture them for thy lusts? That when you are following the world with most eager desires, forgetting the world to come, and the change that is a little before you, conscience might cry out to you, Is Christ and salvation no more worth than so? That when you are next spending the Lord's day in idleness or vain sports, conscience might tell you what you are doing. In a word, that in all your neglects of duty, your sticking at the supposed labour or cost of a godly life, yea, in all your cold and lazy prayers and performances, conscience might tell you how unsuitable such endeavours are to the reward; and that Christ and salvation should not be so slighted.

I will say no more but this at this time. It is a thousand pities that when God hath provided a Saviour for the world, and when Christ hath suffered so much for their sins, and made so full a satisfaction to justice, and purchased so glorious a kingdom for his saints, and all this is offered so freely to sinners, to lost, unworthy sinners, even for nothing, that yet so many millions should everlastingly perish because they make light of their Saviour and salvation, and prefer the vain world and their lusts before them. I have delivered my message, the Lord open your hearts to receive it. I have persuaded you with the word of truth and soberness; the Lord persuade you more effectually, or else all this is lost. Amen.

THE

Grand Question RESOLVED,

What we must do to be *SAVED*.

INSTRUCTIONS

FOR A

𝕳𝖔𝖑𝖞 𝕷𝖎𝖋𝖊:

BY
The Late Reverend Divine,
Mr. *RICHARD BAXTER*.

Recommended to the Bookseller a few days before his Death, to be immediately Printed for the good of Souls.

Acts 16. 30.
Sirs, What must I do to be Saved.

LONDON:
Printed for *Tho. Parkhurst*, at the *Bible* and *Three Crowns* in *Cheap-side*, 1692.

THE GREAT CASE RESOLVED, HOW TO BE CERTAINLY SAVED.

Instructions for a Holy Life
I. THE NECESSITY, REASON, AND MEANS OF HOLINESS.
II. THE PARTS AND PRACTICE OF A HOLY LIFE.
For personal direction and for family instruction.
With two short Catechisms and Prayers.

READER,

IGNORANT persons cannot remember long and many words, nor understand a brief style and few words. This maketh it impossible to write a Catechism that shall not be unsuitable either to the understanding or the memory of such. I must therefore desire the Teacher to make up the unavoidable defect, by opening the meaning,—especially of the Catechisms,—to the children and servants, when they have learned and say the words. Read the Instructions often to them and press all as you go, on their affections. For, the bare words without a present guide may else be all lost.

I. The necessity, reason, and means of Holiness.

1. To keep up the resolutions of the converted. And
2. To instruct those in families that need them.

Though the saving of souls be a matter of inexpressible importance,[1] yet—the Lord have mercy upon them!—what abundance are there that think it not worthy of their serious

---

[1] Mark 8: 36; Matthew 6: 33; Job 21: 14; 22: 17; Psalm 1: 2–3; 14: 12.

enquiry, nor the reading of a good book, one hour in a week! For the sake of these careless slothful sinners, I have here spoken much in a little room, that they may not refuse to read and consider so short a lesson, unless they think their souls worth nothing. Sinner! As thou wilt shortly answer it before God, deny not to God, to thyself and me, the sober pondering and faithful practising these few directions:—

I. Begin at home, and know thyself. Consider what it is to be a man.[1] Thou art made a nobler creature than the brutes. They serve thee, and are governed by thee; and death ends all their pains and pleasures. But thou hast reason to rule thyself and them; to know thy God, and foresee thy end, and know thy way, and do thy duty. Thy reason, and free-will, and executive power, are part of the image of God upon thy nature: so is thy dominion over the brutes, as, under him, thou art their owner, their ruler, and their end. But thy holy wisdom, and goodness, and ability, is the chief part of his image on which thy happiness depends. Thou hast a soul that cannot be satisfied in knowing, till thy knowledge reach to God himself:[2] nor can it be disposed by any other; nor can it or the societies of the world, be well governed according to its nature, without regard to his sovereign authority and without the hopes and fears of joy and misery hereafter;[3] nor can it be happy[4] in anything but seeing and loving and delighting in this God as he is revealed in the other world. And is this nature given thee in vain? If the nature of all things be fitted to its use and end,[5] then it must be so with thine.

II. By knowing thyself then, thou must needs know *that there is a God*:[6] and that he is thy maker and infinite in all perfections;

---

[1] Psalm 8: 4–6; Genesis 1: 26–7; 9: 6; Colossians 3: 10.
[2] John 17: 3; 1 John 4: 6–7; Jeremiah 9: 24.
[3] Luke 12: 4–5.
[4] Psalm 16: 5–11.
[5] Isaiah 45: 18.
[6] Psalm 14: 1; Genesis 1: 1; Revelation 1: 8; Romans 1: 19–20; Psalm 46: 10; 9: 10; 100 and 23; 19: 1–3; 47: 7; Ezekiel 18: 4; Genesis 18: 25; Malachi 1: 6.

and that he is thy Owner, thy Ruler and thy Felicity or End. He is mad that seeth not that such creatures have a cause or maker: and that all the power and wisdom and goodness of the world, is caused by a power and wisdom and goodness which is greater than that of all the world. And who can be our Owner but he that made us? And who can be our highest Governor but our Owner, whose infinite power wisdom and goodness maketh him only fit thereto? And if he be our Governor, he must needs have laws, with rewards for the good and punishments for the bad; and must judge and execute accordingly. And if he be our chiefest Benefactor, and all that we have is from him, and all our hope and happiness is in him, nothing can be more clear than that the very nature of man doth prove that in hope of future happiness, he should absolutely assign himself to the will and disposal of this God, and that he should absolutely obey him,[1] and that he should love and serve him with all his power: it being impossible to love, obey and please that God too much who is thus our cause, our end, our all.

III. By knowing thus thyself and God, it is easy to know what primitive holiness and godliness is. Even this hearty, entire and absolute resignation of the soul to God, as the infinite power, wisdom, and goodness: as our Creator, our Owner, Governor, and Felicity or End: fully submitting to his disposal, obeying his laws, in hope of his promised rewards and fear of his threatened punishments: and loving and delighting in himself and all his appearances in the world: and desiring and seeking the endless right and enjoyment of him in heavenly glory, and expressing these affections in daily prayer, thanksgiving and praise. This is the use of all thy faculties, the end and business of thy life, the health and happiness of thy soul. This is that holiness or godliness which God doth so much call for.

IV. And by this it is easy to know what *a state of sin and ungodliness*

---

[1] Matthew 22: 37; Jeremiah 5: 22; 2 Corinthians 5: 8–9; Titus 2: 14; 2 Corinthians 8: 5; 6: 16–18; 1 Peter 2: 9; Psalm 10; 37: 4; 40: 8; Colossians 3: 1–2; Matthew 6: 20–21; 2 Corinthians 4: 17–18.

is.[1] Even the want of all this holiness, and the setting of carnal self instead of God. When men are proudly great and wise and good in their own eyes, and would dispose of themselves and all their concernments, and would rule themselves and please themselves, according to the fleshly appetite and fancy: and therefore love most the pleasures and profits and honours of the world as the provision to satisfy the desires of the flesh: and God shall be no further loved, obeyed, or pleased than the love of fleshly pleasures will give leave, nor shall have anything but what the flesh can spare: this is a wicked, a carnal, an ungodly state; though it break forth in various ways of sinning.

V. By this, *experience may tell you that all men*[2]—yea all till grace renew them—are in this ungodly miserable state: though only the Scripture tells us how this came to pass. Though all are not fornicators nor drunkards nor extortioners nor persecutors nor live not in the same way of sinning; yet selfishness and pride and sensuality and the love of worldly things, ignorance and ungodliness are plainly become the common corruption of the nature of man; so that their hearts are turned to the world from God, and filled with impiety, filthiness and injustice; and their reason is but a servant to their senses; and their mind and love and lip is carnal;[3] and this carnal mind is enmity to the holiness of God, and cannot be subject to his law. This corruption is hereditary, and is become, as it were, a nature to us, being the mortal malady of all our natures. And it is easy to know that such an unholy, wicked nature, must needs be loathsome to God and unfit for the happy enjoyment of his love, either here or in the life to come:[4] for what communion hath light with darkness?

VI. Hence then it is easy to see what grace is needful to a man's

---

1 Psalm 14: 1; Hebrews 12: 14; Romans 8: 12–13; John 3: 34; 5: 6; 1 John 2: 15–16; Romans 13: 14–15; 6: 16; Luke 18: 23; 14: 26, 33.
2 Romans 3; Psalm 14; Ephesians 2: 2–3; Romans 5: 12, 17, 39; John 3: 6.
3 Romans 8: 5–7.
4 Psalm 4: 3; 2 Corinthians 6: 14, 17.

salvation. So odious a creature, such an unthankful rebel that is turned away from God and set against him, and defiled with all this filth of sin, must needs be both renewed and reconciled,[1] sanctified and pardoned, if ever he will be saved. To love God and be beloved by him and to be delighted herein, in the might of his glory, is the heaven and happiness of souls: and all this is contrary to an unholy state. Till men have new and holy hearts, they can neither see God nor love him nor delight in him nor take him for their chief content: for the flesh and world have their delight and love. And till sin be pardoned,[2] and God is reconciled to the soul, what joy or peace can it expect from him whose nature and justice engageth him to loathe and punish it?

VII. And experience will tell you *how insufficient you are for either of these two works yourselves:*[3] *to renew your souls or to reconcile them unto God.* Will a nature that is carnal resist and overcome the flesh and abhor the sin which it most dearly loveth? Will a worldly mind overcome the world? When custom hath rooted your natural corruptions, are these easily rooted up? O how great and hard a work is it to cause a blind unbelieving sinner to set his heart on another world and lay up all his hopes in heaven, and to cast off all the things he seeth for that God and glory which he never saw. And for a hardened, worldly, fleshly heart to become wise and tender and holy and heavenly, and abhor the sin which it most fondly loveth! And what can we do to satisfy justice and reconcile such a rebel soul to God?

VIII. Nature and experience having thus acquainted you with your sin and misery, and what you want, will further tell you that *God*[4] *doth not yet deal with you according to your deserts.* He giveth you life, and time, and mercies, when your sins had forfeited all these. He obligeth you to repent and turn unto him. And therefore

---

1 Psalm 32: 1–2; 1 Corinthians 6: 11; Titus 2: 14; 3: 5–7; Hebrews 14: 14 (? sic); Matthew 5: 8.
2 Romans 5:1–3.
3 Psalm 97: 7–8, 15; 1 Corinthians 2: 11, 21; Hebrews 14: 12 (? sic); 2 Peter 1: 3.
4 Acts 14: 27; 17: 24–28; Romans 1: 19, 20; 2: 4; Job 33: 14–25; Matthew 12: 42, 43.

experience telling you that there is some hope, and that God hath found out some way of shewing mercy to the children of wrath, reason will command you to enquire of all that are fit to teach you what way of remedy God hath made known. And as you very soon discover that the religion of heathens and Mahometans is so far from shewing the true remedy that they are part of the disease itself: so you may learn that a wonderful Person[1] the Lord Jesus Christ, hath undertaken the office of being the Redeemer and Saviour of the world: and that he who is the eternal Word and Wisdom of the Father, hath wonderfully appeared in the nature of man, which he took from the virgin Mary, being conceived by the Holy Ghost: and that we might have a Teacher sent from Heaven[2] infallibly and easily to acquaint the world with the will of God and the unseen things of life eternal: how God bare witness of the Truth by abundant, open and uncontrolled miracles:[3] how he conquered Satan and the world,[4] and gave us an example of perfect righteousness[5] and underwent the scorn and cruelty of sinners, and suffered the death of the cross as a sacrifice for our sins to reconcile us unto God: how he rose again the third day and conquered death, and lived forty days longer on earth, instructing his apostles and giving them commission to preach the Gospel to all the world, and then ascended bodily into heaven, while they gazed after him: how he is now in heaven, both God and man in one Person, the Teacher and King and High-priest of his Church. Of him must we learn the way of life: by him must we be ruled as the physician of souls. All power is given him in heaven and in earth. By his sacrifice and merits and intercession must we be pardoned and accepted with the Father: and only by him must we come to God. He hath procured and established a covenant of

---

1   Isaiah 9: 6, 7; 53; John 3: 16, 19; 1: 3–4; 3: 2.
2   John 1: 18.
3   Acts 2: 22; Hebrews 2: 3–4.
4   Matthew 4.
5   1 Peter 2: 22–25; Matthew 26: 27–28; Acts 1; Hebrews 4; Ephesians 1: 22, 23; Romans 5: 1, 3, 9; Hebrews 8: 9, 13; 8: 6–7; 7: 25; 1 John 5: 10, 12; John 5: 22; 3: 18–19; Matthew 25.

grace, which baptism is the seal of: Even that God will in him be our God and reconciled Father, and Christ will be our Saviour, and the Holy Ghost will be our Sanctifier, if we will unfeignedly consent; that is if penitently and believingly we give up ourselves to God the Father, Son and Holy Ghost, in these resolutions. This covenant in the tenor of it is a deed of gift, of Christ and pardon and salvation to all the world: if by true faith and repentance they will turn to God. And this shall be the law according to which he will judge all that hear it at the last: for he is made the judge of all, and will raise all the dead, and justify his saints and judge them unto endless joy and glory, and condemn the unbelievers, impenitent and ungodly,[1] unto endless misery. The soul alone is judged at death, and body and soul at the resurrection. This Gospel the apostles preached to the world; and that it might be effectual to man's salvation, the Holy Ghost was first given to inspire the preachers of it,[2] and enable them to speak in various languages, and infallibly to agree in One, and to work many great and open miracles to prove their word to those they preached to. And by this means they planted the Church;[3] which ordinary ministers must increase and teach and oversee, to the end of the world, till all the elect be gathered in. And the same Holy Spirit hath undertaken it as His work[4] to accompany this Gospel and by it to convert men's souls, illuminating and sanctifying them; and by a secret regeneration[5] to renew their natures and bring them to that knowledge and obedience and love of God which is the primitive holiness for which we were created and from which we fell. And thus by a Saviour and a Sanctifier must all be reconciled, and renewed that will be glorified with God in heaven. All this you may learn from the Sacred Scriptures which were written

---

1 Luke 16.
2 Acts 2; John 17: 23.
3 Matthew 28: 19–20; Acts 14: 23; Acts 20; 26: 17- 18.
4 Romans 8: 9.
5 Titus 3: 5, 6; John 13: 5–6.

by the inspiration of the Holy Spirit[1] and sealed by multitudes of open miracles,[2] and contain the very image and superscription of God, and have been received and preserved by the Church as the certain word of God, and blessed by him through all generations, to the sanctifying of many souls.

IX. When you understand all this it is time for you to look home[3] and understand now *what state your souls are in*. That you were made capable of holiness and happiness, you know: that you and all men are fallen from God and holiness and happiness unto self and sin and misery, you know: that you are so far redeemed by Christ, you know, as to have a pardoning and saving covenant tendered you, and Christ and mercy offered to your choice. But whether you are truly penitent believers and renewed by the Holy Ghost and so united unto Christ, this is the question yet unresolved, this is the work that is yet to do, without which there is no salvation, and if thou die before it is done, woe to thee that ever thou wast a man! Except a man be regenerated by the Spirit[4] and converted and made a new creature, and of carnal be made spiritual, and of earthly be made heavenly, and of selfish and sinful be made holy and obedient to God, he can never be saved, no more than the devil himself can be saved. And if this be so—as nothing is more sure—I require thee now, who readest these words, as thou regardest thy salvation, as thou wouldst escape hell-fire and stand with comfort before Christ and his angels at the last, that thou soberly consider whether reason command thee not to try thy state: whether thou art thus renewed by the Spirit of Christ or not,[5] and to call for help to those that can advise thee[6] and follow on the search till thou know thy case. And if thy soul be a stranger to this sanctifying work, whether reason command

---

1 2 Timothy 3: 16.
2 Hebrews 2: 3–4.
3 2 Corinthians 13: 5; Psalm 4: 4; 2 Peter 1: 10.
4 John 3: 5; 2 Corinthians 5: 17; Romans 8: 7–9; Philippians 3: 18–20.
5 Acts 16: 14.
6 Acts 2: 37; 16: 30; 11: 33; 2 Corinthians 6: 1–2; Revelation 2: 7.

thee not, without any delay, to make out to Christ, and beg his Spirit, and cast away thy sins, and give up thyself entirely to thy God, thy Saviour and Sanctifier, and enter into his covenant, with a full resolution never to forsake him; to deny thyself and the desires of the flesh and this deceitful, transitory world, and lay out all thy hopes on heaven, and speedily, whatever it cost thee, to make sure of the felicity which hath no end? And darest thou refuse this when God and conscience do command it? And further I advise you,

X. Understand how it is that *Satan hindereth souls from being sanctified*, that you may know how much to resist his wiles. Some he deceiveth by malicious suggestions that holiness is nothing but fancy or hypocrisy:[1] and God and death and heaven and hell were fancies, this might be believed. Some he debaucheth by the power of fleshly appetite and lust, so that their sins will not let their reason speak: some he keepeth in utter ignorance by the evil education of ignorant parents and the negligence of ungodly soul-murdering teachers:[2] some he deceiveth by worldly hopes, and keepeth their minds so taken up with worldly things, that the matters of eternity can have but some loose and uneffectual thoughts, or as bad as none: some are entangled in ill company,[3] so make a scorn of a holy life, and feed them with continual diversions and vain delights: and some are so hardened in their sin[4] that they are even past feeling, and neither fear God's wrath nor care for their salvation, but hear these things as men asleep, and nothing will awake them. Some are discouraged with a conceit that godliness is a life so grievous,[5] sad and melancholy, that rather than endure it they will venture their souls, come on it what will–as if it were a grievous life to love God and hope

---

1 Acts 24: 14; 28: 22; 24: 5–6.
2 Malachi 2: 7–9; Hosea 4: 9.
3 Proverbs 13: 20.
4 Ephesians 4: 18–19.
5 Malachi 1: 13.

for endless *joys*; and a pleasant life to love the world and sin, and live within a step of hell!—Some that are convinced do put off their conversion with delays, and think it's time enough hereafter: and are purposing and purposing till it be too late, and life and time and hope be ended.[1] And some that see there is a necessity of holiness are cheated by some dead opinion or names or shews and images of holiness:[2] either because they hold a strict opinion or because they are baptized with water and observe the outward parts of worship: and perhaps because they offer God a great deal of lip-service and lifeless ceremony, which never savoured of a holy soul. Thus deadness, sensuality, worldliness and hypocrisy do hinder millions from sanctification and salvation.

XI. If ever thou wouldest be saved, *oppress not reason by sensuality or diversions*: but sometimes retire for sober consideration.[3] Distracted and sleepy reason is unuseful. God and conscience have a great deal to say to thee: which in a crowd of company and business thou art not fit to hear. It is a doleful case[4] that a man who hath a God, a Christ, a soul, a heaven, a hell to think of, will allow them none but running thoughts, and not once in a week bestow one hour in man-like serious consideration of them.[5] Sure thou hast no greater things to mind. Resolve then sometimes to spend half an hour in the deepest thoughts of thy everlasting state.

XII. *Look upon this world and all its pleasures as a man of reason, who foreseeth the end*: and not as a beast that liveth by sense or present objects.[6] Do I need to tell thee, man, that thou must die? Cannot carcases and dust instruct thee to see the end of earthly

---

[1] Matthew 25: 3, 8, 12; 24: 43, 44.
[2] John 8: 39, 42, 44; Romans 3: 1–2; Galatians 4: 29; Matthew 13: 19–22; 15: 2–3, 6; Galatians 1: 1.
[3] Psalm 4: 4; Haggai 1: 5; Deuteronomy 32: 7–29.
[4] Isaiah 1: 3.
[5] Job 34: 27; Jeremiah 23: 20; Psalm 119: 59.
[6] 2 Corinthians 4: 8; Deuteronomy 32: 29; 1 John 2: 17; 1 Corinthians 7: 31; Luke 12: 19–20; John 14: 1–2; 1 Thessalonians 5: 13.

glory and all the pleasures of the flesh? Is it a controversy whether thy flesh must shortly perish? And wilt thou yet provide for it before thy soul? What a sad farewell must thou shortly take of all that worldlings sell their souls for! And O how quickly will this be! Alas! man, the day is even at hand: a few days more and thou art gone! and darest thou live unready, and part with heaven for such a world as this?

XIII. And then think soberly on the life to come:[1] what it is for a soul to appear before the living God and be judged to endless joy or misery! If the devil tempt thee to doubt of such a life, remember that nature and Scripture and the world's consent, and his own temptations are witnesses against him. O man canst thou pass one day in company or alone in business or in idleness, without some sober thoughts of everlastingness? Nothing more sheweth that the hearts of men are asleep or dead than that the thoughts of endless joy or pain, so near at hand, constrain them not to be holy and overcome not all the temptations of the flesh as toys and inconsiderable things.

XIV. *Mind well, what mind most men are of when they come to die!*[2] Unless it be some desperate forsaken wretch do they not all speak well of a holy life? And wish that their lives had been spent in the most fervent love of God and strictest obedience to his laws? Do they then speak well of lust and pleasures and magnify the wealth and honours of the world? Had they not rather die as the most mortified saints, than as careless, fleshly worldly sinners? And dost thou see and know this, and yet wilt thou not be instructed to be wise in time?

XV. *Think well what manner of men these were whose names are now honoured for their holiness.*[3] What manner of life did St Peter and St Paul, St Cyprian, St Augustine, and all other saints and martyrs live? Was it a life of fleshly sports and pleasures? Did they

---

1 Luke 12: 4; Ecclesiastes 12: 7; 2 Peter 3: 11; 2 Corinthians 4: 18; Philippians 3: 18, 20.
2 Numbers 23: 10; Matthew 25: 8; 8: 21–22; Proverbs 1: 28–29.
3 Matthew 23: 29–33; Hebrews 11: 38; John 8: 39.

deride or persecute a holy life? Were they not more strictly holy than any that thou knowest? And is he not self-condemned that honoureth the names of saints and will not imitate them?

XVI. Think what the difference is *between a Christian and an heathen*.[1] You are loath to be heathens or infidels. But do you think a Christian excelleth them but in opinion? He that is not holier than they, is worse, and shall suffer more than they.

XVII. Think what the difference is *between a godly Christian and an ungodly*.[2] Do not all the opposers of holiness among us yet speak for the same God and Christ and Scripture: and profess the same creed and religion, with those whom they oppose? And is not this Christ the author of our holiness, and this Scripture the commander of it? Search and see, whether the difference be not this, that the godly are serious in their profession, and the ungodly are hypocrites, who hate and oppose the practise of the very things which themselves profess: whose religion serveth but to condemn them while their lives are contrary to their tongues.

XVIII. Understand what the devil's policy is by *raising so many sects and factions and controversies about religion in the world*:[3] even to make some think that they are religious because they can prate for their opinions, or because they think their party is the best, because their faction is the greatest or the best; the uppermost or the suffering side. And to turn holy, edifying conference into vain jangling; and to make men atheists—suspecting all religion and true to none—because of men's diversity of minds. But remember that [the] Christian religion is but one, and a thing easily known by its ancient rule; and the universal church containing all churches, is but one. And if carnal interest or opinions so distract men that one party saith `We are all the Church,' and another saith 'It is we'—as if the kitchen were all the house or one town or village

---

1 Matthew 10: 15; Romans 2; Acts 10: 34–5.
2 Romans 2: 28–29; Matthew 25: 28; Luke 19: 22; Acts 24: 15; Galatians 4: 29.
3 Ephesians 4: 14; Acts 20: 30; 1 Corinthians 11: 19; 2 Timothy 4: 3; 2: 14, 16; 1 Timothy 1: 5–6; Titus 3: 9; Ephesians 4: 3 etc.; 1 Corinthians 12; Matthew 12: 25; Romans 2: 12, 27–29.

all the kingdom—wilt thou be mad with seeing this distraction? Hearken sinner, all those sects in the Day of Judgment shall concur as witnesses against thee if thou be unholy: because however else they differed,[1] all of them that are Christians professed the necessity of holiness and subscribed to that Scripture which requireth it. Though thou canst not easily resolve every controversy thou may'st easily know the true religion, it is that which Christ and his apostles taught, which all Christians have professed, which Scripture requireth: which is first pure and then peaceable:[2] most spiritual, heavenly, charitable, and just.

XIX. *Away from that company*[3] *which is sensual*, and an enemy to reason, sobriety and holiness, and consequently to God, themselves and thee. Can they be wise for thee that are foolish for themselves? Or friends to thee that are undoing themselves? Or have any pity on thy soul when they make a jest of their own damnation? Will they help thee to heaven who are running so furiously to hell? Chuse better familiars if thou woulds't be better.

XX. *Judge not of a holy life by hearsay*, for it cannot so be known.[4] Try it awhile and then judge as thou findest it. Speak not against the things thou knowest not. Hadst thou but lived in the love of God, and the lively belief of endless glory, and the delights of holiness, and the fears of hell but for one month or day: and with such a heart hadst cast away thy sin[5] and called upon God and ordered thy family in a holy manner, especially on the Lord's day, I dare boldly say experience would constrain thee to justify a holy life.[6] But yet I must tell thee it is not true holiness if thou but try it with exceptions and reserves.[7] If therefore God hath convinced thee that this is his will and way, I adjure thee as in

---

1 Galatians 1: 7–8; Matthew 28: 20.
2 James 3: 17.
3 Ephesians 5: 11; Proverbs 23: 20; 2 Corinthians 6: 17–18; Psalm 15: 4; Deuteronomy 13: 3.
4 John 5: 40; Luke 14: 29–30; John 6: 35, 37, 45.
5 Isaiah 55: 6–7.
6 Matthew 11: 19.
7 Luke 14: 33.

his dreadful presence, that thou delay no longer[1] but resolve, and absolutely give up thyself to God as thy heavenly Father, thy Saviour and thy Sanctifier, and 'make an everlasting covenant with him,' and then he and all his mercies will be thine: his grace will help thee and his mercy pardon thee: his ministers will instruct thee and his people pray for thee and assist thee: his angels will guard thee and his Spirit comfort thee: and when flesh must fail and thou must leave this world, thy Saviour will then receive thy soul and bring it into the participation of his glory: and he will raise thy body and justify thee before the world and make thee equal to the angels: and thou shalt live in the sight and love of God and in the everlasting pleasures of his glory. This is the end of faith and holiness. But if thou harden thy heart and refusest mercy[2] everlasting woe will be thy portion, and then there will be no remedy.

And now, Reader, I beg of thee and I beg of God on my bended knees that these few words may sink into thy heart and that thou wouldest read them over and over again and bethink thee as a man that must shortly die. Whether any deserve thy love and obedience more than God? And thy thankful rememberance more than Christ? And thy care and diligence more than thy salvation? Is there any felicity more desirable than heaven? Or any misery more terrible than hell? Or anything so regardable as that which is everlasting? Will a few days' fleshly pleasures pay for the loss of heaven and thy immortal soul? Or will thy sin and thy prosperity be meet at death and in the day of judgment? If thou art a man, and as ever thou believest that there is a God and a world to come, and as thou carest for thy soul, whether it be saved or damned, I beseech thee, I charge thee, think of these things! think of them once a day at least! think of them with thy most sober, serious thoughts! Heaven is not a May-game and hell is not a flea-biting!

---

1   Revelation 22: 17; John 1: 12; Revelation 2 and 3; 1 John 5: 12, 13; Psalm 34: 7; Psalm 73: 26; Matthew 25; Luke 20: 39; Hebrews 2: 3; 1 Thessalonians 2: 12.

2   Luke 19: 27; Proverbs 29: 1 and 1: 10, etc.

Make not a jest of salvation or damnation! I know thou livest in a distracted world where thou mayest hear some laughing at such things as these, and scorning at a holy life, and fastening odious reproaches on the godly, and merrily drinking and playing and feasting away their time, and then saying that they will trust God with their souls and hope to be saved without so much ado! But if all these men do not change their minds and be not shortly down-in-the-mouth, and would not be glad to eat their words, and wished that they had lived a holy life, though it had cost them scorn and suffering in the world, let me bear the shame of a deceiver for ever. But if God and thy conscience bear witness against thy sin and tell thee that a holy life is best, regard not the gain-sayings of a bedlam-world, which is drunk with the delusions of the flesh. But give up thy soul and life to God by Jesus Christ in a faithful covenant! Delay no longer, man, but resolve, resolve immediately, resolve unchangeably: and God will be thine and thou shalt be his for ever. Amen. Lord have mercy on this sinner and so let it be resolved by thee in him.

II. The Parts and Practice of a holy life for personal and family instructions.

All is not done when men have begun a religious life.[1] All trees that blossom prove not fruitful, and all fruit comes not to perfection. Many fall off who seemed to have good beginnings; and many dishonour the name of Christ, by their scandals and infirmities. Many do grieve their teachers' hearts and lamentably disturb the Church of Christ, by their ignorance, errors, self-conceitedness, unruliness, headiness, contentiousness, sidings and divisions: insomuch that the scandals and the feuds of Christians are[2] the great impediments of the conversion of the infidel and heathen world, by the exposing Christianity to their contempt and scorn,

---

[1] 1 Corinthians 1: 25; Hebrews 4: 1; 2 Peter 22: 22; 1 Corinthians 3; Galatians 3 and 4; Matthew 13: 41; 18: 7.

[2] Philippians 3: 18–19; Acts 20: 30.

as if it were but the error of men as unholy and worldly and proud as others, that can never agree among themselves. And many by their passions and selfishness are a trouble to their families and neighbours where they live. And more by their weaknesses and great distempers, are snares, vexations and burdens to themselves. Whereas Christianity in its true constitution is a life of such holy light and love,[1] such purity and peace, such fruitfulness and heavenliness, as, if it were accordingly shewed forth in the lives of Christians, would command admiration and reverence from the world and do more to their conversion than swords or words alone can do: and it makes Christians useful and amiable to each other and their lives a feast and pleasure to themselves. I hope it may prove some help to those excellent ends and to the securing men's salvation, if in a few, sound experienced directions I open to you the duties of a Christian life.

I. *Keep still the true form of Christian doctrine, desire and duty, orderly printed on your minds.*[2] that is, understand it clearly and distinctly and remember it, I mean the great points of religion contained in Catechisms. You may still grow in the clearer understanding of your Catechisms, if you live an hundred years. Let not the words only but the matter, be as familiar in your minds as the rooms of your house are. Such solid knowledge[3] will establish you against seduction and unbelief and will be still within you a ready help for every grace and every duty, as the skill of an artificer is for his work. And for want of this when you come among infidels or heretics, their reasonings may seem unanswerable to you, and shake if not overthrow your faith. And you will easily err in lesser points and trouble the Church with your dreams and wranglings. This is the calamity of many professors, that while they will be most censorious judges in every controversy about Church-matters they know not well the doctrine of the Catechism.

---

1   Matthew 5: 16; 1 Peter 2: 18; 2 Corinthians 1: 21.
2   2 Timothy 1: 13; 3: 7; Hebrews 5: 12; Philippians 1: 9; Romans 15: 14.
3   Ephesians 4: 13–14; Colossians 1: 9; 2: 2; 3: 10; 1 Timothy 6: 4.

II. *Live daily by faith on Jesus Christ[1] as the Mediator between God and you.* Being well-grounded in the belief of the Gospel and understanding Christ's office, make use of him still in all your wants. Think on the fatherly love of God, as coming to you through him alone: and of the Spirit as given by him your head: and of the covenant of grace as enacted and sealed by him: and of the ministry as sent by him: and of all times and helps and hopes as procured and given by him. When you think of sin and infirmity and temptations, think also of his sufficient, pardoning, justifying and victorious grace. When thou thinkest of the world, the flesh and the devil, think how he overcometh them. Let his doctrine and the pattern of his most perfect life, be always before you as your rule. In all your doubts and fears and wants go to him in the Spirit and to the Father by him and him alone. Take him as the root of your life and mercies, and live as upon him and by his life; and when you die resign your soul to him that they may be with him 'where he is and see his glory.' To live as Christ and use him in every want and address to God, is more than a general confused believing in him.

III. *To believe in the holy Ghost as to live and work by him, as the body doth by the soul.*[2] You are not baptized into his name in vain;[3] but too few understand the sense and reason of it. The Spirit is sent by Christ for two great works. 1. To the apostles and prophets to inspire them infallibly to preach the Gospel[4] and confirm it by miracles and leave it on record for following ages in the Holy Scriptures. 2. To all his members[5] to illuminate and sanctify them to believe and obey this sacred doctrine—beside his common gift to many to understand and preach it. The Spirit having first indited the Gospel doth by it first regenerate and after govern, all

---

1 John 17: 3; Ephesians 3: 17–18; Matthew 28: 19; Ephesians 1: 22, 23; 4: 6, 16; Romans 5; 2 Corinthians 12: 9; John 16: 33; 1 John 5: 4; Hebrews 4: 14, 16, etc.
2 Galatians 5: 16, 25.
3 Matthew 28: 19.
4 John 16: 13; Hebrews 2: 34.
5 1 Corinthians 12: 12–13; Romans 8: 9, 13; John 3: 5–6.

true believers. He is not now given us for the revealing of new doctrines but to understand and obey the doctrine revealed and sealed by him long ago.[1] As the sun doth by its sweet and discreet influence both give and cherish the natural life of things, sensitive and vegetative: so doth Christ by his Spirit our spiritual life.[2] As you do no work but by your natural life you should do none but by your spiritual life. You must not only believe and love and pray by it, and manage all your calling by it: for 'holiness to the Lord' must be written upon all. All things are sanctified to you because you being sanctified to God devote all to him and use all for him; and therefore must do all in the strength and conduct of the Spirit.

IV. *Live wholly upon God as all in all.*[3] as the first efficient, principal dirigent[4] and final cause of all things. Let faith, hope and love be daily feeding on him. Let 'our Father which art in heaven' be first inscribed on your hearts that he may seem most amiable to you and you may boldly trust him, and filial love may be the spring of duty. Make use of the Son and the Spirit to lead you to the Father: and of faith in Christ to kindle and keep alive the love of God. God's love is our primitive holiness and especially called, with its fruits our sanctification' which 'faith in Christ' is but a means to. Let it be your principal end in studying Christ, to see the goodness, love and amiableness of God in him. A condemning God is not so easily loved as a gracious, reconciled God. You have so much of the Spirit as you have love to God. This is the proper gift of the Spirit to all the adopted sons of God, to cause them with filial affection and dependence to cry 'Abba Father.' Know not, desire not, love not any creature but purely as subordinate to God. Without him, let it be nothing to you, but as the glass

---

[1] 2 Timothy 3: 15–16; Jude 19–20.
[2] Ezekiel 36: 27; Isaiah 44: 3; Romans 8: 1, 5; 1 Corinthians 6: 11; Zechariah 14: 20.
[3] 1 Corinthians 10: 31; Romans 11: 36; 2 Corinthians 5: 7–8; 1 John 3: 1; Romans 5: 1–3; Matthew 22: 37; Ephesians 1: 6; 2 Corinthians 5: 19; Galatians 4: 4–6.
[4] Sic: = 'director.' C.

without the face or scattered letters without the sense or as the corps without the soul. Call nothing prosperity or pleasure but his love:[1] and nothing adversity or misery but his displeasure and the cause and the fruits of it. When anything would seem lovely and desirable which is against him, call it 'dung.'[2] And hear that man as Satan and the serpent[3] that would entice you from him; and count him but vanity, a worm and dust, that would affright you from your duty to him. Fear him much but love him more. Let love be the soul and end of every duty.[4] It is the end and reason of all the rest: but it hath no end or reason but its object. Think of no other heaven and end and happiness of man but love the final act and God the final object. Place not your religion in anything but the love of God, with its means and fruits. Own no grief, desire or joy but a mourning, a seeking and a rejoicing love.

V. *Live in the belief and hopes of heaven, and seek it as your part and end*; and daily delight your souls in the forethoughts of the endless sight and love of God.[5] As God is seen on earth but as in a glass so is he proportionably enjoyed. But when mourning, seeking love hath done, and sin and enemies are overcome, and we behold the glory of God in heaven, the delights of love will then be perfect. You may desire more on earth than you may hope for. Look not for a kingdom of this world, nor for Mount Zion in the wilderness. Christ reigneth on earth—as Moses in the camp—to guide us to the Land of the promise. Our perfect blessedness will be when the kingdom is delivered up to the Father and God is all in all. A doubt, or a strange, heartless thought of heaven, is water cast on the sacred fire, to quench your holiness and your joy. Can you travel one whole day to such an end, and never think of the place that you are going to? Which must be

---

1 Psalm 30: 5; 63: 3.
2 Philippians 3: 7–8.
3 Matthew 16: 13.
4 2 Thessalonians 3: 5; 2 Corinthians 13: 14.
5 Colossians 3: 1–4; Matthew 6: 19–21; 2 Corinthians 4: 17–18; 7; Luke 12: 20; Hebrews 6: 20; 1 Corinthians 15: 28; Ephesians 4: 6; 1: 23; Philippians 3: 18, 20; Psalm 73: 25–26; John 18: 36.

intended[1] in every righteous act—either notedly or by the ready unobserved act of a potent habit. When earth is at the best it will not be heaven. You live no further by faith, like Christians, than you either live for heaven in seeking it or else upon heaven in hope and joy.

VI. *Labour to make religion your pleasure and delight.* Look oft to God, to heaven, to Christ, to the Spirit, to the promises, to all your mercies. Call over your experiences, and think what matter of high delight is still before you, and how unseemly it is, and how injurious to your profession for one that saith he hopeth for heaven, to live as sadly as those that have no higher hopes than earth. How should that man be filled with joy, who must live in the joys of heaven for ever! Especially rejoice when the messengers of death do tell you that your endless joy is near. If God and heaven with all our mercies in the way, be not reason enough for a joyful life, there can be none at all. Abhor all suggestions which would make religion seem a tedious, irksome life. And take care that you represent it not so to others; for you will never make them in love with that which you make them not perceive to be delectable and lovely. Not as the hypocrite, by forcing and framing his religion to his carnal mind and pleasure: but bringing up the heart to a holy suitableness to the pleasures of religion.

VII. *Watch as for your souls against this flattering, tempting world:*[2] especially when it is represented as more sweet and delectable than God and holiness and heaven. This world with its pleasures, wealth and honours, is it that is put in the balance by Satan, against God and holiness and heaven: and no man shall have better than he chooseth and prefereth. The bait taketh advantage of the brutish part when reason is asleep: and if by the help of sense it get the

---

1 Psalm 1: 2–3; : 84: 2, 10; 63: 3, 5; 37: 4; 91: 19; 119: 47, 70; Isaiah 58: 14; Psalm 112: 1; Romans 14: 17; 5: 1, 3, 5; 1 Peter 1: 8; Matthew 5: 11, 12; Psalm 32: 11.

2 Galatians 6: 14; 1 John 2: 15–16; James 1: 27; 4: 4–5; 1 John 5: 4–5; Romans 12: 2; Galatians 1: 4; Titus 2: 12; Matthew 19: 24; Luke 12: 16–21; 16: 25; James 1: 11; 5: 1–4; Luke 8: 14; Hebrews 11: 26.

throne, the beast will ride and rule the man: and reason becomes a slave to sensuality. When you hear the serpent, see his sting and see death attending the forbidden fruit. When you are rising look down and see how far you have to fall! His reason as well as faith, is weak, who for such fools-gawds as the pomp and vanities of this world, can forget God and his soul and death and judgment, heaven and hell, yea and deliberately command them to stand by. What knowledge or experience can do good on that man who will venture so much for such a world, which all that have tried it, call vanity at the last? How deplorable then is a wordling's case! Oh fear the world when it smileth or seems sweet and amiable. Love it not if you love your God and your salvation.

VIII. *Fly from temptations and crucify the flesh and keep a constant government over your appetite and senses.*[1] Many who had no designed, stated vice or worldly interest, have shamefully fallen by the sudden surprise of appetite and lust. When custom hath taught those to be greedy and violent, like a hungry dog or a lusting boar, it is not a sluggish wish or purpose that will mortify or rule them. How dangerous a case is that man in who hath so greedy a beast continually to restrain! that if he do but neglect his watch an hour, is ready to run him headlong into hell! Who can be safe that standeth long on so terrible a precipice? The tears and sorrows of many years may perhaps not repair the loss which one hour or act may bring. The case of David and many others, are dreadful warnings. Know what it is you are most in danger of: whether lust and idleness or excess in meats or drinks or play: and there set your strongest watch for your preservation. Make it your daily business to mortify that lust, and scorn that your brutish sense or appetite should conquer reason. Yet trust not purposes alone: but away from the temptation. Touch not, yea look not on the tempting bait: keep far enough off if you desire to be safe. What miseries come from small beginnings! Temptation leads to

---

[1] Romans 8: 1, 13; Galatians 5: 24; Romans 13: 14; Galatians 5: 17; Jude 8, 23; 2 Peter 2: 10; Ephesians 2: 3; 1 Peter 2: 11; Matthew 6: 13; 26: 41; Luke 8: 13.

sin, and small sins to greater, and those to hell. And sin and hell are not to be played with. Open your sin or temptation to some friend, that shame may save you from danger.

IX. *Keep up a constant, skilful government over your passions and your tongues.*[1] To this end keep a tender conscience, which will smart when in any of these you sin. Let holy passions be well-ordered; and selfish, carnal passions, be restrained. Let your tongues know their duties to God and man[2] and labour to be skilful and resolute in performing them. Know all the sins of the tongue, that you may avoid them: for your innocency and peace do much depend on the prudent government of your tongues.

X. *Govern your thoughts with constant skilful diligence.*[3] In this, rigid habits and affections will do much by inclining them unto good. It's easy to think on that which we love. Be not unfurnished of matter for your thoughts to work upon: and often retire yourselves for serious meditation. Be not so solitary and deep in musings as to over-stretch your thoughts and confound your minds or take you off from necessary converse with others. But be sure that you be considerate and dwell much at home, and converse most with your consciences and your God, with whom you have the greatest business. Leave not your thoughts unemployed or ungoverned, scatter them not abroad upon impertinent vanities! O that you knew what daily business you have for them. Most men are wicked, deceived and undone, because they are inconsiderate and dare not or will not, retiredly and soberly use their reason : or use it but as a slave in chains in the service of their passion, lust and interest. He was never wise or good or happy, who was not soberly and impartially considerate. How to be good, to do good and finally enjoy good, must be the sum of all your thoughts. Keep them

---

1 James 1: 19; 3: 17; 1 Peter 3: 4; Matthew 5: 5; Ephesians 4: 2, 3; Colossians 3: 12.
2 James 1: 26; 3: 5–6; Psalm 34: 13; Proverbs 18: 21.
3 Deuteronomy 15: 9; 2 Corinthians 10: 5; Genesis 6: 5; Psalm 10: 4; 94: 19; 119: 113; Proverbs 12: 5; 15: 26; Psalm 119: 59; Proverbs 30: 32; Jeremiah 4: 14; Deuteronomy 32: 29.

first holy, then charitable, clean and chaste. And quickly check them when they look towards sin.

XI. *Let time be exceeding precious in your eyes, and carefully and diligently redeem it.*[1] What haste doth it make! and how quickly will it be gone! and then how highly will it be valued when a minute of it can never be recalled! O what important business have we for every moment of our time, if we should live a thousand years! Take not that man to be well in his wits or to know his God, his end, his work or his danger, who hath time to spare. Redeem it not only from needless sports and plays and idleness and curiosity and compliment and excess of sleep and chat and worldliness: but also from the entanglements of lesser good which would hinder you from greater. Spend time as men that are ready to pass into another world, where every minute must be accounted for; and it must go with us for ever as we lived here. Let not health deceive you into the expectation of living long, and so into a senseless negligence. See your glass running and keep a reckoning of the expense of time: and spend it just as you would review it when it is gone.

XII. *Let the love of all in their several capacities, become as it were your very nature:*[2] and doing them all the good you can be very much of the business of your lives. God must be loved in all his creatures, his natural image on all men and his spiritual image on his saints. Our neighbour must be loved as our natural selves, that is, our natural neighbour as our natural self, with a love of benevolence: and our spiritual neighbour as our spiritual self, with a love of complacence. In opposition to complacence we may hate our sinful neighbour, as we must ourselves, much more. But in opposition to benevolence we must neither hate ourselves,

---

1 Ephesians 5: 16; John 14: 1–2; Acts 17: 21; 1 Corinthians 7: 29; 2 Corinthians 6: 2; John 9: 4; Luke 19: 42, 44; Psalm 39: 4; Matthew 25: 10, 12.

2 1 Timothy 1: 5–6; Matthew 19: 19; Romans 13: 10; 1 John 1: 16; Ephesians 4: 2, 15–16; Colossians 2: 2; 1: 4; 1 Timothy 6: 11; James 3: 17; Philippians 2: 1–2; 1 Thessalonians 4: 9; John 13: 35; Matthew 5: 44–45; 1 Corinthians 13; James 4: 11; Galatians 6: 10; Titus 2: 14; Philippians 2: 20–21; Romans 15: 1, 3.

our neighbour or our enemy. O that men knew how much of Christianity doth consist in love and doing good. With what eyes do they read the Gospel who see not this in every page? Abhor all that selfishness, pride and passion which are the enemies of love: and those opinions and factions and censurings and back-bitings, which would destroy it. Take him that speaketh evil of another to you without a just cause and call, to be Satan's messenger, entreating you to hate your brother or to abate your love. For to persuade you that a man is bad is directly to persuade you so far to hate him. Not that the good and bad must be confounded: but love will call none bad without constraining evidence. Rebuke back-biters. Hurt no man and speak evil of no man; unless it be not only just but necessarily to some greater good. Love is lovely: they that love shall be beloved; hating and hurting makes men hateful. "Love thy neighbour as thyself," and "do as thou wouldst be done by," are the golden rules of our duty to men: which must be deeply written on your hearts. For want of this there is nothing so false, so bad, so carnal which you may not be drawn to think or say or brethren. Selfishness and want of love do as naturally tend to ambition and covetousness, and thence to cruelty against all that stand in the way of their desires, as the nature of a wolf to kill the lambs. All factions and contentions and persecutions in the world, proceed from selfishness and want of charity. Devouring malice is the devilish nature. Be as zealous in doing good to all as Satan's servants are in hurting. Take it as the use of all your talents, and use them as you would hear of it at last. Let it be your business and not a matter on the by: especially for public good and men's salvation. And what you cannot do yourselves, persuade others to. Give them good books: and draw them to the means which are most like to profit them.

XIII. *Understand the right terms of Church-communion*: especially the unity of the universal church and the universal communion which you must hold with all the parts and the difference between the Church as visible and invisible. For want of these how woeful are our divisions! Read oft 1 Corinthians 12, and Ephesians iv: 1–17; John 17: 21–23; Acts 4: 32; 2: 42; 1 Corinthians 1: 10–13; 3: 3, 12–13; Romans 16: 17; Philippians 2: 1–4; 1 Thessalonians 5: 12–13; Acts 20: 30; 1 Corinthians 11: 19; Titus 3: 10; James 3; Colossians 1: 4; Hebrews 10: 25; Acts 8: 12–13, 37; 1 Corinthians 1: 2, 13; 3: 3–4; 11: 18, 21. Study these well. You must have union and communion in faith and love with all the Christians in the world. And refuse not local communion when you have a just call so far as they put you not on sinning. Let your usual meeting be with the purest church, if you lawfully may—and still respect the public good-but sometimes occasionally communicate with defective, faulty churches, so be it they are true Christians and put you not on sin: that so you may show that you own them as Christians, though you disown their corruptions. Think not your presence maketh all the faults of ministry, worship or people to be yours—for then I would join with no Church in the world. Know that as the mystical church consisteth of heart-covenanters, so doth the Church as visible consist of verbal-covenanters, which make a credible profession of consent: and that nature and scripture teacheth us to take every man's word as credible, till perfidiousness forfeit his credit: which forfeiture must be proved, before any sober profession can be taken for an insufficient title. Grudge not then at the communion of any professed Christian in the Church visible[1]—though we must do our part to cast out the obstinately impertinent by discipline: which, if we cannot do, the fault is not ours. The presence of hypocrites is no hurt but oft a mercy to the sincere. How small else would the Church seem in the world! Outward privileges belong to outward covenanters and inward mercies to the sincere. Division is wounding and tends to death.[2] Abhor it if you love the Church's welfare or your own. 'The wisdom from above is first pure then peaceable.' Never separate what God conjoineth. It is the earthly, sensual, devilish

---

[1] Matthew 13: 29, 41.
[2] John 16: 2; 1 Corinthians 1: 10; Romans 16: 17; James 3: 14–18.

wisdom which causeth bitter envying and strife and confusion and every evil word. 'Blessed are the peace-makers.'

XIV. *Take heed of pride and self-conceitedness in religion.*[1] If once you over-value your own understandings, your crude conceptions and gross mistakes will delight you as some supernatural light; and instead of having compassion on the weak, you will be unruly and despisers of your guides and censorious contemners of all that differ from you, and persecutors of them if you have power, and will think all intolerable that take you not as oracles and your word as law. Forget not that the Church hath always suffered by censorious, worldly professors on the one hand—and O what divisions and scandals have they caused!—as well by the profane and persecutors on the other. Take heed of both: and when contentions are afoot be quiet and silent and not too froward, and keep up a zeal for love and peace.

XV. *Be faithful and conscionable in all your relations.* Honour and obey your parents and other superiors. Despise not and resist not government. If you suffer unjustly by them, be humbled for those sins, which cause God to turn your protectors into afflictors. And instead of murmuring and rebelling against them, reform yourselves and then commit yourselves to God. Princes and pastors I will not speak to: subjects and servants and children, must obey their superiors as the officers of God.

XVI. *Keep up the government of God in your families.*[2] Holy families must be the chief preservers of the interest of religion in the world. Let not the world turn God's service into a customary, lifeless form. Read the scripture and edifying books to them; talk with them seriously about the state of their souls and everlasting life; pray with them fervently; watch over them diligently; be angry against sin and meek in your own cause; be examples of wisdom,

---

[1] 1 Timothy 3: 6; Colossians 2: 18; 1 Corinthians 8: 1; 4: 6; 1 Timothy 6: 4; 1 Peter 5: 5; James 3: 1, 17; Ephesians 5–6; Colossians 3–4; Romans 13: 1, 7; 1 Peter 2: 13, 15.

[2] *Command* 4; Joshua 24: 15; Deuteronomy 6: 6–8; Daniel 6.

holiness and patience; and see that the Lord's day be spent in holy preparation for eternity.

XVII. *Let your callings be managed in holiness and laboriousness.*[1] Live not in idleness; be not slothful in your work be you bound or free; in the sweat of your brows you must eat your bread, and labour the six days that you may have to give to him that needeth: slothfulness is sensuality as well as filthier sins. The body that is able must have fit employments as well as the soul, or else body and soul will fare the worse; but let all be but as the labour of a traveller, and aim at God and heaven in all.

XVIII. *Deprive not yourself of the benefit of an able, faithful pastor,*[2] to whom you may open your case in secret, or at least of a holy faithful friend:[3] and be not displeased at their free reproofs.[4] Woe to him that is alone! How blind and partial we are in our own cause! and how hard it is to know ourselves without an able, faithful helper! You forfeit this great mercy when you love a flatterer, and angrily defend your sin.

XIX. *Prepare for sickness, sufferings and death.*[5] Over-value not prosperity nor the favours of man. If selfish man prove false and cruel to you, even those of whom you have deserved best, marvel not at it, but pray for your enemies, persecutors and slanderers, that God would turn their hearts and pardon them. What a mercy is it to be driven from the world to God, when the love of the world is the greatest danger of the soul! Be ready to die and you are ready for anything. Ask your hearts seriously, what is it that I shall need at a dying hour? And let it speedily be got ready and not be to seek in the time of your extremity.

XX. *Understand the true method of peace of conscience*: and judge not

---

[1] Hebrews 13: 5; *Command* 4; 2 Thessalonians 3: 10, 12; 1 Thessalonians 4: 7; 1 Timothy 5: 13; Proverbs 31; 1 Corinthians 7: 29.
[2] Malachi 2: 7.
[3] Ecclesiastes 4: 10, 11.
[4] Proverbs 12: 1; 15: 30–31; Hebrews 3: 13.
[5] Luke 12: 40; 2 Peter 1: 10; Philippians 1: 21, 23; Jeremiah 9: 4–5; Matthew 7: 4–5; 2 Corinthians 5: 1–2, 4, 8.

the state of your souls upon deceitful grounds. As presumptuous hopes do keep men from conversion and embolden them to sin: so causeless fears do hinder our love and praise of God, by obscuring his loveliness: and they destroy our thankfulness and our delight in God, and make us a burden to ourselves and a grievous stumbling-block to others. The general grounds of all your comfort are (1) the gracious nature of God[1] (2) the sufficiency of Christ[2] and (3) the truth and universality of the promise[3] which giveth Christ and life to all, if they will accept him. But this acceptance is the proof of your particular title, without which these do but aggravate your sin. Consent to God's covenant is the true condition and proof of your title to God as your Father, Saviour and Sanctifier, and so to the saving blessings of the covenant: which consent, if you survive, must produce the duties which you consent to. He that heartily consenteth that God be his God, his Saviour and Sanctifier, is in a state of life. But this includeth[4] the rejection of the world. Much knowledge, and memory, and utterance, and lively affection, are all very desirable. But you must judge your state by none of these, for they are all uncertain. But 1. If God and holiness and heaven have the highest estimation by your practical judgment, as being esteemed best for you: 2. And be preferred in the choice and resolution of your wills and that habitually before all the pleasures of the world: 3. And be first and chiefly sought in your endeavours: this is the infallible proof of your sanctification. Christian, upon long and serious study and experience I dare boldly commend these Directions to thee, as the way to God, which will end in blessedness. The Lord resolve and strengthen thee to obey them. This is the true constitution of Christianity: this is true godliness: and this is to be religious indeed: all this

---

1 Exodus 34: 6.
2 Hebrews 7: 25.
3 John 4: 42; John 3: 16; 1 Timothy 4: 10; 2: 4; Matthew 28: 19–20; Revelation 22: 17; Isaiah 55: 1–3. 6–7.
4 Luke 14: 26, 33; 1 John 2: 15; Matthew 6: 19, 20–1, 33; Colossians 3: 1, 2; Romans 8: 1, 13.

is no more than to be seriously such as all among us in general would prefer to be. This is the religion which must difference you from hypocrites, which must settle you in peace and make you an honour to your profession and a blessing to those that dwell about you. Happy is the land, the church, the family, which doth consist of such as these! These are not they that either persecute or divide the church or that make their religion a servant to their policy, to their ambitious designs or fleshly lusts; nor that make it the bellows of sedition or rebellion or of an envious hurtful zeal or a pistol to shoot at the upright in heart. These are not they that have been the shame of their profession, to hardening of ungodly men and infidels, and that have caused the enemies of the Lord to blaspheme. If any man will make a religion of or for his lusts: of Papal tyranny, or Pharisaical formality, or of his private opinions, or of proud censoriousness and contempt of others: and of faction and unwarrantable separations and divisions and of standing at a more observable distance from common professors of Christianity than God would have them, or yet of pulling up the hedge of discipline and laying Christ's vineyard common to the wilderness—the storm is coming when this religion founded on the sand will fall "and great will be the fall thereof." When the religion which consisteth in faith and love to God and man, in mortifying the flesh and crucifying the world, in self-denial, humility and patience in sincere obedience and faithfulness in all relations, in watchful self-government, in doing good and in a divine and heavenly life, though it will be hated by the ungodly world—shall never be a dishonour to your Lord nor deceive or disappoint your soul.

A Short Catechism

Quest. I. What is the Christian Religion?

Ans. The Christian Religion is the baptismal-covenant made and kept: wherein God the Father, Son and Holy Ghost, doth give Himself to be our reconciled God and Father, our Saviour and Sanctifier: and we believingly give up ourselves accordingly to Him, renouncing the "flesh, the world and the devil." Which covenant is to be oft renewed, specially in the sacrament of the Lord's Supper.

Quest. 2. Where is our covenant-part and duty fullier opened?

Ans. 1. In the Creed, as the sum of our belief.

2. In the Lord's Prayer, as the sum of our desires.

3. And in the Ten Commandments (as given us by Christ, with the Gospel-explanations) as the sum of our practice. Which are as followeth—

The Creed.

I believe in God the Father Almighty, Maker of heaven and earth; and in Jesus Christ his only Son our Lord, who was conceived by the Holy Ghost, born of the virgin Mary, suffered under Pontius Pilate, was crucified, dead, and buried: he descended into hell; the third day he rose again from the dead; he ascended into heaven, and sitteth on the right hand of God the Father Almighty; from thence he shall come to judge the quick and the dead. I believe in the Holy Ghost; the holy catholic church; the communion of saints; the forgiveness of sins; the resurrection of the body; and the life everlasting. Amen.

The Lord's Prayer.

Our Father, which art in heaven, Hallowed be thy name. Thy kingdom come. Thy will be done on earth, as it is in heaven. Give us this day our daily bread, and forgive us our debts, as we forgive our debtors. And lead us not into temptation; but deliver us from evil: For thine is the kingdom, and the power, and the glory, for ever. Amen.

The Ten Commandments.

I. I am the Lord thy God, which have brought thee out of the land of Egypt, out of the house of bondage. Thou shalt have no other gods before me.

II. Thou shalt not make unto thee any graven image, or any likeness of any thing that is in heaven above, or that is in the earth beneath, or that is in the water under the earth: Thou shalt not bow down thyself to them, nor serve them: for I the Lord thy God am a jealous God, visiting the iniquity of the fathers upon the children unto the third and fourth generation of them that hate me; and shewing mercy unto thousands of them that love me, and keep my commandments.

III. Thou shalt not take the name of the Lord thy God in vain: for the Lord will not hold him guiltless that taketh his name in vain.

IV. Remember the Sabbath-day, to keep it holy. Six days shalt thou labour, and do all thy work: but the seventh day is the sabbath of the Lord thy God: in it thou shalt not do any work, thou, nor thy son, nor thy daughter, thy man-servant, nor thy maid-servant, nor thy cattle, nor thy stranger that is within thy gates: for in six days the Lord made heaven and earth, the sea, and all that in them is, and rested the seventh day: wherefore the Lord blessed the sabbath-day, and hallowed it.

V. Honour thy father and thy mother: that thy days may be long upon the Land which the Lord thy God giveth thee.

VI. Thou shalt not kill.

VII. Thou shalt not commit adultery.

VIII. Thou shalt not steal.

IX. Thou shalt not bear false witness against thy neighbour.

X. Thou shalt not covet thy neighbour's house, thou shalt not covet thy neighbour's wife, nor his man-servant, nor his maid-servant, nor his ox, nor his ass, nor any thing that is thy neighbour's.

Quest. 3. Where is the Christian Religion most fully opened and entirely contained?

Ans. In the Holy Scriptures, especially of the New Testament: where, by Christ and his Apostles and Evangelists, inspired by His Spirit, the history of Christ and His Apostles is sufficiently delivered, the promises and doctrines of faith are perfected, the covenant of grace more clearly opened and church-offices, worship and discipline established: on the understanding whereof the strongest Christians may increase while they live on earth.

The explained Profession of the Christian Religion.

I. I believe that there is One God, an infinite Spirit of life, understanding and will: perfectly powerful, wise and good: the Father, the Word and the Spirit, the Creator, Governor and End of all things: our absolute Owner, our most just Ruler and our most gracious Benefactor and most amiable Lord.

II. I believe that man being made in the image of God, an embodied spirit of life, understanding and will, with holy suavity, wisdom and love, to know and love and serve his Creator here and for ever, did by wilful sinning fall from his God, his holiness and innocency, under the wrath of God, the condemnation of his Law, and the slavery of the flesh, the world and the devil. And that God so loved the world that He gave His only Son to be their Redeemer, who being God and one with the Father, took our nature and became man: being conceived of the Holy Ghost, born of the virgin Mary, called Jesus Christ, who was perfectly holy [and] sinless, fulfilling all righteousness, overcame the devil and the world and gave Himself a sacrifice for our sins, by suffering a cursed death on the cross, to ransom us and reconcile us unto God: and was buried and went among the dead: the third day He rose again, having conquered death. And He fully established the covenant of grace, that all that truly repent and believe shall have the love of the Father, the grace of the Son and the communion of the Holy Spirit; and if they love God and obey him sincerely to the death, they shall be glorified with him in heaven for ever; and the unbelievers, impenitent and ungodly shall go to everlasting punishment. And having commanded his Apostles to preach the Gospel to all the world and promised His Spirit, He ascended into heaven: where He is the glorified Head over all things to the Church and our prevailing Intercessor with the Father: who will there receive the departed souls of the justified: and at the end of this world will come again and rouse all the dead and will judge all according to their works and justly execute his Judgment.

III. I believe that God the Holy Spirit was given by the Father and the Son, to the prophets, apostles and evangelists, to be their infallible guide in preaching and recording the doctrine of salvation: and the witness of its certain truth, by his manifold Divine operations: and to question, illuminate and sanctify all the believers, that they may renounce the flesh, the world and the devil. And all that are thus sanctified are one holy and catholic Church of Christ and must live in holy communion and have the pardon of their sins and shall have everlasting life.

The *Covenant or Covenants.*—Believing in God the Father, Son and Holy Spirit, I do perfectly, absolutely and resolutely give up myself to Him, my Creator and reconciled God and Father, my Saviour and Sanctifier: and repenting of my sins I renounce the devil, the world and the sinful desires of the flesh: and denying myself and taking up my cross, I consent to follow Christ the captain of my salvation, in hope of His promised grace and glory.

A short Catechism for those that have learned the first.

Quest. 1. What do you believe concerning God?

Ans. There is one only God, an infinite Spirit of life, understanding and will, most perfectly powerful, wise and good: the Father, the Word and the Spirit: the Creator, Governor and End of all things: our absolute Owner, our most just Ruler, and our most gracious and most amiable Father.

Quest. 2. What believe you of the Creation, and the nature of man and the law which was given to him?

Ans. God created all the world: and made man in his own image, an embodied spirit of life, understanding and will, with holy liveliness, wisdom and love: to know and love serve his Maker here and for ever: and gave him the inferior creatures for his use; but forbad him to eat of the tree of knowledge upon pain of death.

Quest. 3. What believe you of man's fall into sin and misery?

Ans. Man being tempted by Satan, did by wilful sinning fall from his holiness, his innocency, and his happiness, under the justice of God, the condemnation of his Law, and the slavery of the flesh, the world and the devil; whence sinful, guilty and miserable natures are propagated to all mankind: and no mere creature is able to deliver us.

Quest. 4. What believe you of man's Redemption by Jesus Christ?

Ans. God so loved the world that He gave His only Son to be their Saviour: Who being God and One with the Father, took our nature and became man: being conceived by the Holy Ghost, born of the virgin Mary and called Jesus Christ: Who was perfectly holy, without sin, fulfilling all righteousness: and overcame the devil and the world; and gave himself a sacrifice for our sins, by suffering a cursed death on the Cross to ransom us and reconcile us unto God: and was buried and went among the dead: the third day He rose again, having conquered death; and having sealed the New Covenant with His blood, He commanded His apostles and other ministers, to preach the Gospel to all the world: and promised the Holy Ghost: and then ascended into heaven, where He is God and man, the glorified Head over all things to His Church, and our prevailing intercessor with God the Father.

Quest. 5. What is the New Testament or Covenant or law of grace?

Ans. God through Jesus Christ doth freely give to all mankind Himself, to be their reconciled God and Father, the Son to be their Saviour, and the Holy Spirit to be their Sanctifier, if they will believe and accept the gift and will give up themselves to Him accordingly: repenting of their sins and consenting to forsake the devil, the world and the flesh, and sincerely, though not perfectly, to obey Christ and the Spirit to the end, according to the law of nature and the gospel institutions, that they may be glorified in heaven for ever.

Quest. 6. What believe ye of the Holy Ghost?

Ans. God the Holy Ghost was given by the Father and the Son to the prophets, apostles and evangelists, to be their infallible guide in preaching and recording the doctrine of salvation: and the witness of its certain truth by his manifold Divine operations. And He is given to quicken, illuminate and sanctify all true believers, and to save them from the devil, the world and the flesh.

Quest. 7. What believe you of the holy Catholic Church, the communion of saints and the forgiveness of sins?

Ans. All that truly consent to the baptismal covenant, are one sanctified Church or Body of Christ, and have communion in the same spirit of faith and love, and have the forgiveness of all their sins: and all that by baptism sensibly covenant and that continue to profess Christianity and holiness, are the universal visible Church or state: and must keep holy communion with love and peace in the particular Churches: in the doctrine, worship and order instituted by Christ.

Quest. 8. What believe you of the Resurrection and everlasting life?

Ans. At death the souls of the justified go to happiness with Christ, and the souls of the wicked to misery: and at the end of the world Christ will come in glory and will raise the bodies of all men from death and will judge all according to their works: and the righteous shall go into everlasting life where being made perfect themselves, they shall see God and perfectly love and praise Him, with Christ and all the glorified Church: and the rest into everlasting punishment.

Quest. 9. You have told me what you believe: Tell me now what is the full resolution and desire of your will concerning all this which you believe.

Ans. Believing in God the Father, Son and Holy Spirit, I do presently, absolutely and resolutely give up myself to Him, my

Creator and reconciled God and Father, my Saviour and my Sanctifier! And repenting of my sins I renounce the devil, the world and the sinful desires of the flesh. And denying myself and taking up my cross, I consent to follow Christ, the captain of my Salvation: in hope of the grace and glory promised. Which I daily desire and beg as He hath taught me saying Our Father which art in heaven, etc.

Quest. 10. What is the practice which by this covenant you are obliged to?

Ans. According to the law of nature and Christ's institutions I must—desiring perfection—sincerely obey Him in a life of faith and hope and love: loving God as God for Himself above all, and loving myself as His servant, especially my soul, and seeking its holiness and salvation: and loving my neighbour as myself. I must avoid all idolatry of mind and body, and must worship God according to His Word, by learning and meditating on His Word: by prayer, thanksgiving, and praise and use of his Sacrament.[1]

I must not profane but holily use His holy name: I must keep holy the Lord's Day, especially in communion with the Church-assemblies: I must honour and obey my parents, magistrates, pastors and other rulers: I must not wrong my neighbour in thought, word or deed, in his soul, his body, his chastity, estate, right or propriety [=property]: but do him all the good I can: and do as I would be done by: which is summed up in the Ten Commandments 'God spake these words, saying,' etc.

A Prayer for Families in the method of the Lord's Prayer, being but an Exposition of it. Most glorious God, who art power and Wisdom and Goodness itself, the Creator of all things: the Owner, the Ruler and the Benefactor of the world: though by sin, original and natural we were Thy enemies, the slaves of Satan and our flesh, and under Thy displeasure and the condemnation of Thy Law: yet Thy children redeemed by Jesus Christ Thy Son, and regenerated

---

[1] The Lord's Supper and other Church-ordinances are referred to in the VIIIth day's Conference, and more fully in my *Universal Concord*.

by Thy Holy Spirit, have leave to call Thee their reconciled Father. For by Thy covenant of grace Thou hast given them Thy Son to be their Head, their Teacher and their Saviour: and in Him Thou hast pardoned, adopted and sanctified them: sealing and preparing them for Thy celestial kingdom and beginning in them that holy life and light and love which shall be perfected with Thee in everlasting Glory. O with what wondrous love hast Thou loved us, that of rebels we should be made the sons of God! Thou hast advanced us to this dignity that we might be elevated wholly to Thee as Thine own, and might delightfully obey Thee and actively love Thee with all our heart: and so might glorify Thee here and forever.

O cause both us and all Thy churches, and all the world, to hallow Thy great and holy name! and to live to Thee as our ultimate end: that Thy shining image and holy soul may glorify Thy divine perfection.

And cause both us and all the earth to cast off the tyranny of Satan and the flesh and to acknowledge Thy supreme authority and to become the kingdoms of Thee and Thy Son Jesus, by a willing and absolute subjection. O perfect Thy kingdom of grace in ourselves and in the world and hasten the kingdom of glory.

And cause us and thy churches and all people of the earth no more to be ruled by the lusts of the flesh and their erroneous conceits, and by self-will, which is the idol of the wicked: but by Thy perfect wisdom and holy will revealed in Thy laws. Make known Thy Word to all the world and send them the messengers of grace and peace: and cause men to understand, believe and obey the Gospel of salvation, and that with such holiness, unity and love, that the Earth which is now too like hell may be made liker unto heaven: and not only Thy scattered, imperfect flock but those also who in their carnal and ungodly minds do now refuse a holy life and think Thy word and ways too strict, may desire to imitate even the heavenly Church: where Thou art obeyed and loved and praised, with high delight, in harmony and perfection:

And because our being is the subject of our well-being, maintain us in the life which Thou hast here given us, until the work of life be finished: and give us such health of mind and body and such protection and supply of all our wants as shall fit us for our duty and make us contented with our daily bread and patient if we want it. And save us from the love of the riches and honours and pleasures of this world; and the pride, and idleness and sensuality which they cherish. And cause us to serve Thy Providence by our diligent labours, and to serve Thee faithfully with all that Thou givest us. And let us not make provision for the flesh to satisfy its desires and lusts.

And we beseech Thee of Thy mercy, through the sacrifice and propitiation of Thy beloved Son, forgive us all our sins, original and actual, from our birth to this hour: our omissions of duty and committing what Thou didst forbid: our sins of heart and word and deed; our sinful thoughts and affections, our sinful passions and discontents, our secret and our open sins, our sins of negligence and ignorance and rashness: but especially our sins against knowledge and conscience, which have made the deepest guilt and wounds. Spare us O Lord and let not our sins so find us out as to be our ruin: but let us so find them out as truly to repent and turn to Thee! Especially punish us not with the loss of Thy grace! Take not Thy Holy Spirit from us and deny us not Thy assistance and holy operations. Seal to us by that Spirit the pardon of our sins, and lift up the light of Thy countenance upon us and give us the joy of Thy favour and salvation. And let thy love and mercy so fill us not only with thankfulness to Thee: but with love and mercy to our brethren and our enemies, that we may heartily forgive them that do us wrong, as through Thy grace we hope we do. And for the time to come, suffer us not to cast ourselves wilfully into temptations: but carefully to avoid them and resolutely to resist and conquer what we cannot avoid. And O sanctify those inward sins and lusts which are our constant and most dangerous temptations: and let us not be tempted by

Satan or the world, or tried by Thy judgments above the strength which Thy grace shall give us. Save us from a fearless confidence in our own strength. And let us not dally with the snare nor taste the bait nor play with the fire of Thy wrath: but cause us to fear and depart from evil: lest before we are aware we be entangled and overcome and wounded with our guilt and with Thy wrath, and our end should be worse than our beginning. Especially save us from those radical sins of error and unbelief, pride, hypocrisy, hardheartedness, sensuality, slothfulness and the love of the present world and the loss of our love to Thee, to Thy kingdom and Thy ways.

And save us from the malice of Satan and of wicked men and from the evils which our sins would bring upon us.

And as we crave all this from Thee, we humbly render our praises with our future service to Thee! Thou art the king of all the world and more than the life of all the living! Thy kingdom is everlasting! Wise and just and merciful is Thy government. Blessed are they that are Thy faithful subjects. But who hath hardened himself against Thee and hath prospered? The whole creation proclaimeth Thy perfection: But it is to heaven where the blessed see Thy glory and the glory of our Redeemer, where the angels and saints behold Thee, admire Thee, adore Thee, love Thee, and praise Thee with triumphant, joyful songs, the holy, holy, holy God, the Father, Son and Holy Ghost, who was and is and is to come. Of Thee and through Thee and to Thee are all things. To Thee be glory for ever. Amen.

A Short Prayer for Families.

Most glorious, ever-living God, Father, Son and Holy Ghost, infinite in Thy power, wisdom and goodness! Thou art the Author of all the world, the Redeemer of lost mankind, and the Sanctifier of Thine elect! Thou hast made us living, reasonable souls, placed awhile on earth in flesh, to seek and know and love and serve Thee, which we should have done with all our soul and might.

For we and all things are Thine own and Thou art more to us than all the world. This should have been the greatest business care and pleasure of our lives. We were bound to it by Thy Law and invited by Thy love and mercy and the promise of a reward in heaven. And in our baptism we were devoted to this Christian life of faith and holiness, by a solemn covenant and vow. But with grief and shame we do confess that we have been too unfaithful to that covenant and too much neglected the Lord our Father, our Saviour and our Sanctifier, to whom we were devoted. And have too much served the flesh and the world and the devil which we renounced. We have added to our original sin, the guilt of unthankfulness for a Saviour and resisting the Spirit and grace that should have renewed, governed and saved us. We have spent much of our lives in fleshly and worldly vanity and wilfully neglected the greatest work of making a sure preparation for death and judgment and our endless state. In a custom of sinning we have hardened our hearts against Thy Word and warnings and the reproofs of thy ministers and of our consciences that have oft told us of our sin and danger and called us to repent. And now O Lord! our convinced souls confess that we deserve to be forsaken by Thee and left to our own lust and folly and to the deceits of Satan and unto endless misery. But seeing Thou hast given a Saviour to lost man and a pardoning covenant through the merits of Christ, promising forgiveness and salvation to every true, penitent, believer, we thankfully accept Thy offered mercy and penitently bewail our sin and cast our miserable souls upon Thy grace and the sacrifice, merits and intercession of our Redeemer.

Forgive all the sins of our hearts and lives; and as a reconciled Faher take us as Thy adopted children in Christ. O give us Thy renewing Spirit to be in us a powerful and constant author of holy light and love and life, to fit us for all our duty and for communion with Thee and for everlasting life. And to dwell in us as Thy witness and seal of our adoption. Let Him be better to our souls than our souls are to our bodies, teaching us Thy word and will, and bringing all our love and will to a joyful compliance with Thy will and quickening our dull and drowsy hearts to a holy and heavenly conversation. Let Him turn all our sinful pleasures and desires unto the delightful love of Thee and of Thy ways and servants. Save us from the great sins of selfishness pride and worldliness, and give us self-denial, humility and a heavenly mind, that while we are on earth, our hearts may be in heaven, where we hope to live in Thy joyful love and praise, with Christ and all His holy ones for ever. Let us never forget that this life is short and that the life to come is endless: that our souls are precious and our bodies vile and must shortly turn to rottenness and dust: that sin is odious and temptation dangerous and judgment dreadful to unprepared, guilty souls: and that to them a Saviour and His grace and Spirit there is no salvation. Cause us to live as we would die, and let no temptation, company or business, draw us to forget our God and our everlasting state. -

Lord bless the world, and specially these kingdoms, with wise, godly, just and peaceable princes and inferior judges and magistrates; and guide, protect and perfect them for the common good and the promoting of godliness and suppressing of sin. And bless all Churches with able, godly, faithful Pastors, that are zealous lovers of God and goodness and the people's souls. And save the nations and churches from oppressing tyrants and deceivers, and from malignant enemies to serious piety. And cause subjects to live in just obedience and in love and peace. Bless Families with wise, religious governors, who will carefully instruct their children and servants and restrain them from sin and keep them from temptation. Teach children and servants to fear God and honour and obey their governors.

O our Father which art in heaven, let Thy name be hallowed: Let Thy kingdom come: Let Thy will be done on earth as it is in heaven: Give us this day our daily bread: Forgive us our trespasses as we forgive them that trespass against us: Lead us not into temptation but deliver us from evil: for Thine is the kingdom, the power and the glory for ever. Amen.

Before Meal.

Most gracious God, who hast given us Christ and with Him all that is necessary to life and godliness: we thankfully take this our food as the gift of Thy bounty, procured by His merits. Bless it to the nourishment and strength of our frail bodies to fit us for Thy cheerful service. And save us from the abuse of Thy mercies by gluttony, drunkenness, idleness and sinful fleshly lusts, for the sake of Jesus Christ our only Saviour and Lord. Amen.

After Meat.

Most merciful Father, accept of our thanks for these and all Thy mercies: and give us yet more thankful hearts. O give us more of the great mercies proper to Thy children, even Thy sanctifying and comforting Spirit, assurance of Thy love through Christ and a treasure and a heart and conversation in heaven. And bring and keep us in a constant readiness for a safe and comfortable death: for the sake of Jesus Christ our Lord and only Saviour. Amen.

F I N I S

CALAMY ON BAXTER

BY ALAN C. CLIFFORD

Apart from modest attention from nonconformist scholars, Dr Calamy is a largely unsung hero of a depressing period in English church history. While he never had the impact of his hero Richard Baxter (and how many could claim that until George Whitefield appeared in 1735?), admiring Calamy shared most of Baxter's convictions, a good deal of his piety and an equally-strong pastoral and evangelistic commitment. In addition, besides documenting the sacrifice of the ejected ministers of 1662, he perhaps more than any other preacher and theologian transmitted Baxter's wonderful legacy to the eighteenth century and beyond. At a time when frequently-persecuted Protestant Dissent struggled to justify its existence within late Stuart and early Hanoverian society, Dr David Wykes points out that Calamy emerged as the 'Champion of Nonconformity'.[1] His own fascinating autobiography illuminates the period in which he lived. For these reasons, we do well to explore the life and labours of Dr Edmund Calamy.

To start with, Edmund Calamy had a remarkable ancestry. He was the third Edmund in a line beginning with his grandfather (1600–66) whose own Norman French Huguenot father came to England via Guernsey following the St Bartholomew persecution of 1572. A graduate of Pembroke Hall, Cambridge and an eminent

---

[1] *DNB*: David. L. Wykes, 'Calamy, Edmund (1671–1732)', *Oxford Dictionary of National Biography* (Oxford University Press, 2004), (http://www.oxforddnb.com/view/article/4357?docPos=3).

preacher among the Puritans, Edmund I played a prominent part in the Westminster Assembly (1643–9). Our Edmund's father—Edmund II (1634–85)—was born in Bury St Edmunds, Suffolk, his father having previously ministered in Swaffham, Norfolk. Edmund II became Rector of Moreton in Essex, losing his living—as did his father in London—at the time of the Great Ejection (1662). In these momentous times—the Plague of 1665 followed by the Great Fire of London in 1666—Edmund I died. The sight of the devastated city soon brought him to his grave. Our Edmund was born in London in 1671. Then Edmund III's son Edmund IV (1697–1755) also became a minister of the Gospel. Not forgetting Calamy's significant Huguenot origins, he was conscious of his godly pedigree: 'I count it my honour to be descended on ye side both of Father & Mother from the Old Puritans'.[1] Accordingly, his early published sermons indicated that the author was 'E. F. & N.'—Edmundus Filius et Nepos (i.e. Edmund, son and grandson).

Knowing the grace of God early in his life, Edmund's education prepared him for future pastoral service. Robert Tatnal's school in Westminster, then Thomas Doolittle's Academy at Islington led via Thomas Walton's School in Bethnal Green to Merchant Taylors' School after his father's death in 1685. A year later he entered Samuel Cradock's Academy at Wickhambrook near Newmarket, Suffolk. Professing personal conversion at this time, he then 'went to the Lord's Table'. In every respect, he declared: 'I must freely own I can look back on the time spent at Mr Cradock's academy with comfort and pleasure, blessing God for the benefit I there received ... it was no small encouragement to me, to have this good old gentleman, upon his hearing me preach, a good many years after, come and embrace me in his arms, thanking God for the hand he had in my education'.[2]

---

[1] Ibid.

[2] *An Historical Account of My Own Life* (London: Henry Colburn and Richard Bentley, 1830), i. 145 (cited in A. H. Drysdale, 'Dr Edmund Calamy' in *Short Biographies for the People by Various Writers* (London: Religious Tract society, 1890), vii. No. 77, 6).

In 1688, on the advice of the eminent Puritan John Howe (1630–1705), Edmund travelled to the Netherlands with other ministerial students to study at Utrecht. Studying in foreign Reformed institutions was the only way to obtain a higher education, entry to Oxford and Cambridge then being only open to Anglicans. This was a critical year for the future of European Protestantism. In October, Calamy saw William of Orange embark on his enterprise to liberate England from the Catholic designs of James II.

As much as Calamy and his generation valued the rigours of academic training, they were aware of the danger of unsanctified intelligence. Just as Baxter, Howe and others were careful to promote piety as well as sound learning, young Calamy shared their concerns. Besides escaping from a near-fatal accident on Dutch ice, he was aware of the threat of frozen orthodoxy. On leaving Holland for home in 1691, he expressed regret that though there were many English ministerial students at Utrecht,

> ... we had no meetings among ourselves for prayer and Christian converse. Had I not been provided with many good practical books of English divinity, which I read frequently with profit and pleasure, I doubt it would have been worse with me than it was. From my own experience I can heartily recommend all students of theology, while laying in a stock of divinity in speculative way, to read pious and devotional works, so as to have a warmer sense of the things of God on their minds and hearts.[1]

Calamy's concern probably explains why he appreciated worshipping among the Huguenot refugees:

> In the French Church at Utrecht ... there was ... M. Saurin ... a very grave man, and one of great depth of thought; who was for going to the bottom of a subject, and when he had

---

[1] Ibid. 188 (Drysdale, 7).

doctrinally opened it, had a marvellous way of touching the passions.[1]

Returning to London, Edmund met the aged Richard Baxter. This was an important event in his life, as he makes clear:

> I particularly waited on Mr Baxter, who talked freely with me about my good old grandfather, for whom he declared a particular esteem.

Part of this esteem would have related to the 'Amyraldian' (or Davenantian!) convictions articulated by Edmund Calamy I during the sessions of the Westminster Assembly.[2] Edmund continued:

> I several times heard [Mr Baxter] preach, which I remembered not to have done before. He talked in the pulpit with great freedom about another world, like one that had been there, and was come as a sort of an express from thence to make a report concerning it. He was well advanced in years, but delivered himself in public, as well as in private, with great vivacity and freedom, and his thoughts had a peculiar edge. I told him of my design of going to Oxford, and staying sometime there, in which he encouraged me: and towards the end of the year, (Dec. 8) when I was actually there, he died; so that I should never have had an opportunity of seeing, hearing, or conversing with him, had I not done it now.[3]

The chief purpose of Calamy's studies at this time was to settle the question: was he to serve in the Church of England or among the Protestant Dissenters? So, aided by a letter of recommendation from one of his Dutch professors, he availed himself of the facilities of the Bodleian Library, Oxford. Among other works, he read Richard Hooker's *The Laws of Ecclesiastical Polity* (1590). However,

---

[1] *Account of My Own Life*, i. 145.
[2] See Alan C. Clifford, *Atonement and Justification: English Evangelical Theology 1640–1790—An Evaluation* (Oxford: Clarendon Press, 1990/2002), 75.
[3] Calamy, *An Historical Account*, i. 220–1.

as his detailed and comprehensive critique makes clear, Calamy remained totally unimpressed by the author's case for classical Anglicanism.[1] Carefully studying his Bible, 'and particularly the New Testament', he concluded that 'the plain worship of the Dissenters' was 'more agreeable to that, than the pompous way of the Church of England'.[2] William Chillingworth's *The Religion of Protestants* (1638) persuaded him that the Bible alone, rather than man-made confessions of faith (however sound), must be the basis of faith and concord among Christians.[3] Lodging with the Oxford Presbyterian minister Joshua Oldfield, Calamy was encouraged to preach his first sermon. As yet unordained, he felt somewhat intimidated by the event. His hearers included a 'greater number of scholars than usual'. However, our young preacher says "I bless God, however, I was not dashed, but came off pretty well. I discoursed both parts of the day from Heb.2: 3, 'How shall we escape if we neglect so great salvation?' " Speaking of 'the great salvation of the Gospel', he expounded 'the necessity' of 'the satisfaction that our blessed Saviour made for sin by offering up himself as a sacrifice ... according to the common way of our Protestant writers'.[4]

Returning to London in 1692, Calamy accepted a call from Matthew Sylvester's congregation at Meeting-House Court, Blackfriars. He and five other candidates were eventually ordained at Dr Samuel Annesley's Meeting House on 22 June 1694, Dr Daniel Williams—the eminent Presbyterian leader—and five ejected ministers officiating. This was the first public ordination of the Dissenters since the Act of Uniformity (1662). Calamy's first published sermon appeared around this time: *A Practical Discourse concerning Vows: with a special reference to Baptism and the Lord's Supper* (1694). This work, indicates Drysdale, 'proved' a

---

[1] Ibid. 235–46.
[2] Ibid. 224–5.
[3] Ibid. 227–34.
[4] Ibid. 268.

blessing to 'more than his hearers. "If ever any saving impressions have been made upon my soul," writes one, "the reading of your treatise on vows was the great instrument. May I never forget the strong and lively influence it had on me.'"[1]

The following year, Edmund Calamy became assistant to Dr Daniel Williams at Hand Alley, Bishopsgate Street. In the same year (1695) he married Mary Watts, a marriage that proved happy and fruitful until Mary died in 1713. Their eldest son, Edmund IV (d. 1755) was born in 1698.

Having recently commenced a regular and dedicated pastoral ministry in London lasting thirty-eight years, Calamy also embarked on his career as an historian. So, in 1696, he aided Matthew Sylvester in publishing Richard Baxter's *Autobiography: the Reliquiae Baxterianae*. Thereafter, he amazingly found time to preserve and promote the memory of Baxter and the ejected ministers. Believing that Sylvester's devoted yet defective work would be more effective in an edited form, Calamy published *An Abridgement of Mr Baxter's History of His Life and Times with An account of the Ministers ... who were Ejected after the Restoration of King Charles II* (1702). Integral with his ministry, Calamy clearly felt called of God to transmit the heroic faith of Baxter and his brethren: "To let the Memory of these Men Dye is injurious to Posterity".[2] His *Abridgement* involved great courage, and it provoked a storm. At a time of continuing Anglican-inspired hostility to the heirs of the Puritans, this inspiring material marked out Edmund Calamy as 'the Champion of Nonconformity'.[3]

In 1702, Calamy was chosen as one of the Tuesday lecturers at Salters' Hall. Dating from earlier times, these public merchants lectures played a vital role in promoting Christian edification. Calamy's first and highly-impressive contribution was *Divine*

---

[1] Drysdale, *Short Biographies for the People* (London, 1890), 11.
[2] Wykes, *Oxford DNB*.
[3] Ibid.

Mercy Exalted: or Free Grace in its Glory (1703), 'Published at the Request of Many Encouragers of the Lecture'.[1]

That same year, Calamy became the minister of Tothill Street, Westminster. As his influence in the public affairs of the Dissenters began to increase, he was concerned clearly to define the Dissenting Presbyterian position *vis-à-vis* the Anglican Establishment, but without rancour and extremism. Thus, in the manner of Calvin, the Westminster divines and Baxter, and to vindicate the ejected clergy, this English churchman preached and published his *Defence of Moderate Nonconformity* (in three parts, 1703–5). For all his 'moderation', he—as did Baxter before him—presents a cogent and comprehensive biblical demonstration 'that presbyters are by Divine Right the same as Bishops'[2] and that the apostolic meaning of 'bishop' is *not* 'the sense the Church of England gives that word'.[3]

Far from ignoring—in some doctrinaire fashion—that biblical pastoral order is designed to promote practical piety in the lives of God's people, Calamy published Richard Baxter's *Practical Works* in 1707.[4] This was a major publishing event where Calamy was concerned. In his preface, after highlighting the 'valuable treatises of practical divinity published in this country', Calamy states that

> there are no writings of that kind among us, that have more of a true Christian spirit, a greater mixture of judgement and affection, or a greater tendency to revive pure and undefiled religion that have been more esteemed abroad, or more blessed at home for the awakening the secure, instructing the ignorant, confirming the wavering, comforting the dejected, recovering

---

1 *Divine Mercy Exalted*, title page.
2 *Defence of Moderate Nonconformity* (Part I) (London: Thomas Parkhurst, 1703), 71.
3 Ibid. 72.
4 *The Practical Works of the Late Reverend and Pious Mr Richard Baxter*, in Four Volumes (London: Thomas Parkhurst, 1707).

the profane, or improving such as are truly serious, than the Practical Works of this author.[1]

Adept at citing 'opposition' support, Calamy says 'That great man Bishop Wilkins was used to say of Mr Baxter, that if he had lived in the Primitive times he had been One of the Fathers of the Church: what then more fit than a collection of his works, that posterity may be taught to do him justice?'[2]

Before we explore Calamy's edition of Baxter's *Practical Works*, a look at his own theology is appropriate. The best source for this is his little-known and generally-neglected publication, *Divine Mercy Exalted*. Indeed, in a thoroughly dismissive manner, the Unitarian historian Alexander Gordon declared that 'no one reads Calamy's sermons'.[3] Neither does he bother to mention *Divine Mercy Exalted*. Even Dr David Wykes (also a Unitarian), while stating that 'Calamy was Baxterian in theology',[4] fails to mention this most important testimony to Calamy's Baxterian soteriology. The 'sermonic lecture' was clearly intended not only to edify his hearers but to advertise the young minister's commitment to 'Baxterian Calvinism' *vis-à-vis* the prevailing extremes of Arminianism and Owenism. Judging by the title page, it met a widespread need for clarity over many of the most controversial issues of recent history. Indeed, this work is a well-structured, biblically-based and luminously-insightful exposition of the Gospel which repays careful study.

In the preface to *Divine Mercy Exalted*, Calamy reveals his perspective on the subject in hand. In order to express his position, he appeals not to the over-refined orthodoxy of the Westminster Assembly (1643–9) but to the unexaggerated theology of the Synod of Dort (1618). While he often made respectful references to the WCF in later years, Calamy was evidently happier with

---

[1] Ibid. p. iii.
[2] Ibid.
[3] See the article on Calamy in the *DNB* (Oxford: OUP, 1885–1900).
[4] David L. Wykes, 'Calamy, Edmund (1671–1732)', *Oxford DNB*.

the more moderate stances of Dort and of Bishop John Davenant who was one of the British delegates at the Synod:

> I have considered Divine grace as actually discovering itself to sinners, rather than as purposed in the Decree: but he that would see that discussed, and the doctrine of particular election maintained, consistently with a general love of God to the world, would do well to consult the learned and peaceable Bishop Davenant's *Animadversions upon Hoard's Treatise of God's Love to Mankind*; a book which is not valued according to its worth: though one would think it were therefore the more to be regarded in these points, because the worthy author was so considerable a member of the forementioned Synod, in which the controversy about grace and free-will was so distinctly debated.[1]

Perhaps surprisingly, without even a single reference to Richard Baxter, Calamy does what his hero also did—appeal to John Davenant's 'middle way' between 'free will' Arminianism and what became 'limited atonement' Owenism. In the context of these debates, Davenant's *Dissertation on the Death of Christ* (originally in Latin[2]) is well known (even though the Banner of Truth Trust deleted it from their 2005 edition of Davenant's *Exposition of Colossians,* an omission remedied by Dr Digby James of the Quinta Press).[3] However, Calamy's citation of Davenant's lesser-known-work[4] against the Arminian Anglican Samuel Hoard is important in dealing with the predestinarian background to the atoning work

---

1 *Divine Mercy Exalted: or Free Grace in its Glory* (London: Thomas Parkhurst, 1703), pp. iii-iv.

2 *Dissertationes Duae; prima, de Morte Christi; altera, De Praedestinatione et Electione, &c* (Cambridge, 1650). Later published as *An Exposition of the Epistle of St Paul to the Colossians* by The Right Revd John Davenant, D. D., translated from the original Latin; with a life of the Author by Josiah Allport (two volumes, London, 1831).

3 See my Introduction to John Davenant, *A Dissertation on the Death of Christ* (Weston Rhyn: Quinta Press, 2006).

4 *Animadversions written by the Right Rev. Father in God, John, Lord Bishop of Salisbury, upon a treatise intituled, God's Love to Mankind* (Cambridge, 1641).

of Christ. Indeed, Davenant's *Animadversions* is probably the best balanced, albeit brief, biblical exposition of predestination ever written. Besides resolving numerous knotty issues, it provides practical guidance to preachers on how and how not to preach on the subject. In the process of rescuing the Bible's teaching on this subject from Hoard's repeated misrepresentations, Davenant also rescues John Calvin from the unjust aspersions cast on him on account of the doctrine.[1] In short, Davenant's teaching was the perfect Bible-based antidote to a later extremism of the kind Baxter and later Calamy sought to oppose. This was a Gospel stance[2] which could not only claim support from Calvin and many other reformers. Above all, Calamy—like Baxter—believed such was the true teaching of the Holy Scriptures.

We now return to Calamy's edition of *The Practical Works of the Late Reverend and Pious Mr Richard Baxter*, In Four Volumes [folio]. With a Preface; Giving some Account of the Author, and of this Edition of his Practical Works (London, 1707).

Fully-conscious of the importance of the publication, Calamy's enthusiasm is evident in the 'proposal', to which is added a list of thirty-four subscribers. The gracious, courageous and attractive grandeur in the text demands a full quotation:

> AMONG all the great and useful projects of this kind that have been set on foot this age, perhaps there have been none so likely to reach all the desirable purposes this may be serviceable for. Here you have not only a few particular heads of Christian Faith and Practice, but Christianity itself, in its full extent and

---

[1] See *Animadversions*, 26, 39, 42, 64, 96, 99, 135, 139–43, etc.
[2] 'Christ died for all and every singular person, who by repentance and faith in His blood may, according to the tenor of the Gospel, have eternal life given him through Jesus Christ our Lord. And Christ died thus for all, not only because His death was in regard of the worth a sufficient ransom for all and more than all, but because it is God's settled purpose, by Christ's bloodshed to save any man that shall believe truly in Him, and to save no man that continueth an unbeliever. Christ died not to save any few selected ones without their repentance and faith; and Christ died not with an exception or exclusion of any one man in the world from the benefit of salvation, performing the condition of faith and repentance' (ibid. 472–3).

compass, most accurately handled, and at the same time with greatest plainness suited to the meanest capacities, and pressed home upon the consciences of readers with inimitable life and fervour. And how great an advantage must it be to have such an help at hand in families, to which you may have recourse upon all occasions, to clear your judgements in the great Articles of Religion, to ease your minds in the most perplexing cases of conscience, to engage and direct you in the several most important exercises of godliness! You need not fear any danger from hence of being influenced for or against any party of Christians as such: For in all his writings you will find the evidences of a large and truly Christian spirit, too great to be confined to the narrow limits of one or other party; and that noble catholic temper is what he everywhere labours to infuse into his readers: A temper not only most pleasant to the persons themselves in whom it has place, but which at last must heal all the unhappy differences in the Christian world, if ever God have so much mercy for us.[1]

Boosted by Bishop Wilkins' commendation (as noted earlier), and affirming that Baxter's works are 'a treasure of practical divinity as no other part of the Christian Church can furnish [us] with', Calamy uses the Preface to inform the reader about the author. Although Sylvester's edition of the *Reliquiae Baxterianae* (1696) and Calamy's *Abridgement* (1702) had already appeared, Calamy is aware that many might not have access to those publications. What is, in effect, Calamy's second abridgement of Baxter's life, his preface provides a useful overview, not least on account of its brevity. My intention is to select some quotations that highlight Calamy's admiring sense of Richard Baxter's uniqueness as a faithful servant of our Lord Jesus Christ.

After announcing the birth on 12 November 1615 of Puritanism's 'Shropshire lad', Calamy briefly sketched Baxter's

---

1 *Practical Works*, p. xviii.

family connections. Doubtless partly because he was denied access to the English Universities on account of his Dissenting persuasions, Calamy was quick to highlight his hero's largely self-taught academic accomplishments. Encouraged by others, Baxter

> followed his studies with indefatigable earnestness; and soon made such improvements as amazed those that knew, how slender his helps were, and how difficult it is for a man to beat out his way himself. Though he never led an academical life (which he much desired), yet by the divine blessing upon his rare dexterity and diligence, his sacred knowledge (as Dr Bates expressed it in his funeral sermon) was in that degree of eminence, as few in the university ever arrive to'.[1]

More important than Baxter's cerebral brilliance was his spiritual progress:

> His early seriousness was remarkable. Dr Bates tells us, that his father said with tears of joy to a friend, my son Richard I hope was sanctified from the womb: for when he was a little boy in coats, if he heard other children in play speak profane words, he would reprove them, to the wonder of them that heard him. As he grew up, he listened to the instructions of his father, and abhorred those profane sports which were common on the Lord's Days, in the places where he lived, and while the rest were dancing he was employed in religious exercises. He betimes loved his Bible, and was afraid of sinning. He loathed the company of scoffers, and loved religion the better for their reproaches.[2]

Reinforced by health concerns, Baxter's spiritual progress was aided by books of practical piety, notably 'Parson's of *Resolution*, as corrected by Bunny'.[3] Because his precarious health forbad

---

[1] Ibid. p. iv.
[2] Ibid.
[3] Ibid.

any expectation of a long-life, and desiring 'to do some good to ignorant and careless sinners before he died', he entered the ministry, being 'examined and ordained by the Bishop of Worcester'. Baxter commenced his ministry (one might say) as 'a conventional Anglican'. However, after his settlement at Dudley, a book by William Ames persuaded him that Puritanism had a strong case against 'Anglicanism'. Accordingly, after moving to Bridgnorth, 'he neither baptized with the sign of the cross, nor wore the surplice'. Furthermore, he became convinced that diocesan Episcopacy—'the English frame of Church Government'[1]—was of doubtful validity.

Calamy introduces Baxter's famous ministry at Kidderminster with a sense of rhapsody:

> He spent two years at Kederminster [sic] before the Civil War broke out [1642], and above 14 years after, ... He found the place like a piece of dry and barren earth; ignorance and profaneness as natives of the soil were rife among them: But by the blessing of heaven upon his labour and cultivating, the face of paradise appeared there in all the fruits of righteousness. At first rage and malice created him much opposition: but it was soon over, and a special Divine blessing gave his unwearied pains among that people an unexpected success.[2]

At this point, instead of Calamy's paraphrase, I quote Baxter's own gripping account of the town's transformation:

> The congregation was usually full, so that we were fain to build five galleries after my coming thither, the church itself being very capacious, and the most commodious and convenient that ever I was in. Our private meetings also were full. On the Lord's Days there was no disorder in the streets, but you might hear an hundred families singing psalms and repeating sermons as you

---

1 Ibid. p. v.
2 Ibid.

passed through the streets. In a word, when I came thither first there was about one family in a street that worshipped God and called on His name, and when I came away there were some streets where there was not passed one family in the side of a street that did not so, and that did not, by professing serious godliness, give us hopes of their sincerity. And those families which were the worst, being inns and alehouses, usually *some persons* in each house did seem to be religious ...[1]

Continuing with Calamy, Baxter 'had 600 communicants; and there were not above 12 of them, of whose sincerity in religion he had not hopes. There were few families in the whole town that refused to submit to his private catechizing, and personal conferences; and few went away, without some tears, or seemingly serious promises of a godly life'.[2]

The figure of '600 communicants' is worth pausing for. In a town of around 3–4,000 souls and 1800 adults (including the surrounding villages),[3] the scale of the impact of Baxter's ministry becomes clearer. In short, about a third of the population of seventeenth-century Kidderminster made a sincere profession of faith. In terms of the 2011 census which recorded a population of 55,530 in the town,[4] it is virtually impossible to imagine a church building large enough for Baxter's congregation had he lived in our time. Perhaps even the facilities of Kidderminster Town's soccer stadium would struggle to accommodate it!

No less remarkable is the bond of love between Baxter and his congregation. 'In short, so much of the presence of God did Mr Baxter find accompanying him in his work, and so affectionate was his regard to the loving people of that place, that he would not willingly have changed his relation to them for any preferment

---

[1] *Reliquiae Baxterianae*, I, i. §136; Nuttall, 49, 47.
[2] *Practical Works,* p. vi.
[3] Nuttall, 46.
[4] https://en.wikipedia.org/wiki/Kidderminster

in the Kingdom, nor could he without force have been separated from them.'¹

Proceeding beyond the period of the Civil War (which Calamy briefly narrates), neither will I re-visit Baxter's enormous influence on other ministers and churches via the Worcestersire Association except to add some remarks on Baxter's view of church order. On this issue, Calamy says:

> In the controversy about church government, which was then so hotly agitated, Mr Baxter was all along against extremes. He neither fell in with the Erastian, nor Episcopal, nor Presbyterian, nor Independent party entirely; but thought that all of them had so much truth in common among them, as would have made these Kingdoms happy, had it been unanimously and soberly reduced to practice, by prudent and charitable men.²

Calamy's 'entirely' is important. Baxter thought that each party 'had some truths in peculiar ... and each one had their proper mistakes'.³ Towards the end of his life, he declared, 'You could not (except a Catholic Christian) have trulier called me than an Episcopal-Presbyterian-Independent'.⁴

Such a potentially-confusing 'triple label' needs clarification! Looking at the first, Baxter embraced Archbishop Ussher's reduced Episcopacy—with Calvin and Beza's support!⁵ This meant a rejection of the traditional diocesan scheme in favour of a local, 'hands-on' parochial bishop or pastor, a preaching bishop, not a 'remote' church administrator or prelate out of direct touch with parish reality. Baxter believed this was the New Testament idea of a 'bishop'.⁶

Looking at the second 'label', it was not for nothing that Baxter

---

1 *Practical Works*. p. vii.
2 Ibid. p. viii.
3 *Reliquiae Baxterianae*, I, ii, §1.
4 *A Third Defence of the Cause of Peace* (1681), i. 110; see Nuttall, 84.
5 Baxter, *Five Disputations of Church Government* (London, 1659), 344ff.
6 Baxter, *Paraphrase on the New Testament* (London, 1685), note on Acts 20: 17.

was viewed as the English Presbyterian leader. He affirmed the biblical Presbyterian idea that 'presbyter' and 'bishop' were one and the same office.[1] Such pastors were 'presbyter-bishops' or 'elder-overseers'. Hence Judge Jeffreys' jibe that Baxter's concept of a parochial bishop was 'presbyterian cant'.[2] Yet Baxter rejected the idea of 'lay elders'.[3] At Kidderminster, aided by deacons, he and his assistant were the only church elders. He held that synods had a place, not as authoritative courts but as assemblies for fellowship and encouragement.[4] Such 'Presbyterian' ideas found expression in the Worcestershire Association. Regarding the third 'label', he considered that the local church had all rights and privileges under Christ, and that neither diocesan nor synodical power provide validity for the congregation's functions.[5] Thus, from week-to-week, the church at Kidderminster worshipped as a self-functioning congregational community.[6]

Calamy endorsed Baxter's plea for a reduced confessional test at the 1654 'Fundamentals' conference. Contrary to his many critics, he was no friend of anti-trinitarian falsehood.

> Mr Baxter was for offering to the Parliament the Creed, the Lord's Prayer, and the Ten Commandments, as the Fundamentals of Christianity: But the rest were not for so large a bottom, but were for having a greater number of Fundamentals. If he did no other service among them, he at least prevented the running many things so high as might otherwise have been expected.[7]

That said, while Owen was responsible for wording the proposed sixteen articles, this 'minimalist' approach did not prevent him

---

1 Ibid. note on Titus 1: 7.
2 *Autobiography of Richard Baxter,* ed. J. M. Lloyd Thomas (London: J. M. Dent, 1931), 262. Hereinafter, *Autobiography.*
3 Baxter, *Five Disputations,* 5.
4 Baxter, *Five Disputations,* 348; Baxter, *Paraphrase,* note on Ephesians 4: 16.
5 Baxter, *Five Disputations,* 348; Nuttall, 54.
6 Nuttall, 61.
7 *Practical Works,* p. viii. See my *Richard Baxter: The Gospel Truth* (2016), 101–2.

from later producing for the Independents a 'maximal', *ultra-biblical* statement (derived from the *Westminster Confession*) in the *Savoy Declaration* (1658). Baxter obviously lamented Owen's 'over-orthodox' view of imputation.[1]

Calamy also commends Baxter's proposal to reform worship at the Savoy Conference (1661). His *Reformed Liturgy*—a document of sacred, Bible-based eloquence—was an attempt to provide a more biblical alternative to the *Book of Common Prayer* for those who dare not subscribe the latter as in all respects agreeable to Holy Scripture. Even today, for those who dare not imagine Cranmer could be supplanted by anyone, let alone Baxter, Calamy's narrative retains its cogency:

> For the design of [Baxter's] liturgy was not to justle out the old one as it was, where persons were satisfied with it, but to relieve those that durst not use the old one as it was, by helping them to forms taken out of the Word of God. Or suppose we, that the old Liturgy had in the esteem of many fallen short of this new one; others are at a loss to discover why this should appear so preposterous, unless it be unaccountable for persons to prefer a liturgy entirely Scriptural, to one that is made up of human phrases, and some of them justly enough exceptionable.[2]

Calamy makes it clear that Baxter's alternative was not driven by disrespect for Cranmer's *magnum opus*. The 'old liturgy' was an honourable replacement for pre-Reformation forms of worship, drawn up in an era of persecution and martyrdom. It was simply Baxter's desire to build on their legacy. Surely, would not Cranmer *et al* have approved of Baxter's endeavours? Yes, says Calamy:

> Had they risen from the dead, there's good reason to believe they would generally have approved of it; and been so far from

---

[1] See Baxter, *Catholick Communion Defended* (1684), II. 8 and *An End of Doctrinal Controversies* (London: 1691), 266.
[2] *Practical Works*, p. ix.

looking upon it as detracting from them, that they would have applauded it as a good superstructure upon their foundations.[1]

Needless to say, the 'Anglican élite' sought to discredit Baxter's work on grounds of his lack of university education. Apart from Baxter himself not being in the least intimidated by the bishops,[2] Calamy makes the point that the author's brethren at the Savoy Conference had full confidence in his abilities:

> They approving it when they perused it, and joining in the presenting it, made it their own, as sufficiently appears from the Preface prefixed; and some of them [notably Dr Bates and Dr Manton] had academical education, and great applause in the world too, and yet thought not Mr Baxter at all their inferior.[3]

Calamy mentions Baxter's refusal of the 'Bishoprick of Hereford'[4] and his frustration at being denied a return to his beloved people at Kidderminster. Continuing to preach 'up and down occasionally' in London, 'he was fix'd a lecturer with Dr Bates at St Dunstan in Fleet Street ... Here he had a crowded auditory'.[5] Following the Great Ejection (24 August, 1662), including persecution and imprisonment, the authorities did everything to silence Baxter. His ever-popular preaching was considered a dangerous threat to the Restoration order. Although Calamy doesn't mention it, the sadness Baxter must have felt was dispelled by his happy marriage to Margaret Charlton in September 1662.[6] At the time of the Plague (1665), living and preaching at Acton was likely to

---

[1] Ibid.
[2] '... our frequent crossing of their expectations ... had made some of the bishops angry; above all Bishop Morley, who overruled the whole business, ... But that which displeased them most was the freedom of my speeches to them; that is, that I spoke to them as on terms of equality as to the cause, yet with all honourable titles to their persons' (*Autobiography*, 165).
[3] *Practical Works*, p. ix.
[4] Ibid.
[5] Ibid. p. x.
[6] See *Autobiography*, Appendix 2; 'Richard Baxter's Love-story and Marriage', 267ff; also Nuttall, 93ff.

produce another Kidderminster! 'He had so many came to hear him, that he wanted room'.[1] After a six months prison sentence, he moved to Totteridge near Barnet. Legally free to preach during the King's Indulgence (1672), 'He returned to his preaching in the City'.[2] In response to growing public demand for Baxter's preaching, enthusiastic friends built a meeting house in Oxenden Street. He only preached there once, and, providentially being out of town soon after, narrowly escaped arrest. Undaunted, Baxter 'afterwards built another meeting house in St Martin's Parish, but was forcibly kept out of it, by constables and officers'.[3] However, there was some respite from this incessant opposition. A way opened for Baxter to preach when a pastor in Southwark died; 'he upon the invitation of his people preached to them many months in peace'.[4]

When one realises that in all this harassment, Baxter's treatment was accompanied by 'great pain', it is astonishing that he remained unembittered towards the authorities. Yet, this irrepressible servant of Christ received ambiguous treatment, as Calamy makes clear: 'Though he was thus treated all King Charles's reign [1660–85], he yet prayed as heartily for him as any man; and he was often consulted about terms and measures for an union, between the Conformists and the Nonconformists as to which he was ever free to give his sentiments'.[5] In 1674, Baxter (along with his friends Dr William Bates, Dr Thomas Manton and Matthew Poole) was involved in a scheme for comprehension with such 'low church' Latitudinarians as Dr Edward Stillingfleet and Dr John Tillotson. Alas, the 'high church' establishment made sure the scheme would never be approved.

Ever the pastor, in 1685 Baxter published *A Paraphrase on the*

---

1   *Practical Works*, p. xi.
2   Ibid.
3   Ibid.
4   Ibid.
5   Ibid. p. xii.

New Testament with Notes, Doctrinal and Practical. This was intended for 'the Use of religious families, in their daily reading of the Scriptures'. Calamy narrates the well-known impact of this book thus: 'In the reign of King James II [1685–88], Mr Baxter was committed to the King's Bench prison by warrant from the Lord Chief Justice Jeffreys, for his *Paraphrase on the New Testament,* which was called a scandalous and seditious book against the Government. On May 30, 1685, he was brought to his trial'.[1]

Baxter's comments on several texts relating to bishops and liturgy were cited as evidence by the Prosecution. Despite the endeavours of the Defence, 'Jeffreys interrupted his Counsel in pleading for him, and treated Mr Baxter most scornfully'.[2] Indeed, the story is well known. A fuller account of the proceedings is found in Calamy's *Abridgement of Mr Baxter's History.* The racy narrative makes it clear that the Lord Chief Justice wasn't very interested in truth or justice. The sick and aged Baxter—he was nearly 70—was repeatedly shouted down when attempting to speak. Scurrility knew no bounds when Jeffreys abused the saintly Baxter. "This is an old rogue" cried the judge, "and hath poisoned the world with his Kidderminster doctrine!" Baxter was reviled as "an old schismatical knave, a hypocritical villain!" When further attempting to explain his views, the Lord Chief Justice burst forth:

> Richard, Richard, dost thou think we'll hear thee poison the court? Richard, thou art an old fellow, an old knave; thou hast written books enough to load a cart, every one as full of sedition, I might say treason, as an egg is full of meat. Hadst thou been whipped out of thy writing trade forty years ago, it had been happy ...[3]

Strange as it may seem, a report of Baxter's trial by one 'I. C.'

---

1 Ibid.
2 Ibid.
3 See Calamy, *Abridgement of Mr Baxter's History of His Life and Times,* Second edition (London: 1713), 370–1; also *Autobiography,* 262.

was sent to Matthew Sylvester in 1694 during his work on Baxter's papers. For some reason, he appears to have made no use of it in the *Reliquiae* (1696).[1] However, this was remedied by Calamy who included the information in his *Abridgement* (1702, 2nd ed. 1711). While few details of the trial appear in the *Preface* under review, neither is Tillotson's moving letter (1692) to Sylvester referred to, although Baxter's conformist friend—the future Archbishop of Canterbury—is. It is surely appropriate to include an extract from it here:

> Nothing more honourable than when the Reverend Baxter stood at bay, berogued, abused, despised—Never more great than then. Draw this well ... This is the noblest part of his life, & not that he might have been a bishop. The Apostle when he would glory, mentions his labours & stripes & bonds & imprisonments; his troubles, weariness, dangers, reproaches; not his riches & coaches, & honours, & advantages ...'[2]

Duly convicted, Baxter was in prison from June 1685 to November 1686. Eventually, 'His fine was remitted: and November 24, Sir Samuel Astrey sent his warrant to the keeper of the Kings bench to discharge him'. Being allowed to 'reside in London', in February 1687 he moved 'to a house in Charterhouse Yard'.[3] For the remainder of his life, Richard Baxter served alongside Matthew Sylvester. With his own personal touches, Calamy's account of the final years augments those of Sylvester and Bates.

> After his settlement [at Charterhouse Yard], he gave Mr Sylvester (whom he particularly valued, and had a special intimacy with) and his flock, his pains, *gratis*, every Lord's Day in the morning; and every other Thursday morning at a weekly lecture. And thus he continued for about 4 years and a half;

---

1 *Autobiography*, 258.
2 See N. H. Keeble and Geoffrey F. Nuttall, *Calendar of the Correspondence of Richard Baxter* (Oxford: Clarendon Press, 1991), ii. 330 (Letter 1260); also *Autobiography*, 298.
3 *Practical Works*, p. xii.

rejoicing as much as any man in the happy Revolution under the conduct of King William [1688], though he appeared not much in public ... At length his distempers took him off [his ministerial labours], and confined him first to his chamber, and then to his bed. Under sharp pains, he was very submissive to the will of God. And when he was inclined to pray most earnestly for a release, he would check himself and say, *It is not fit for me to prescribe: Lord, when Thou wilt; what Thou wilt; how Thou wilt.* As his end drew near, being often asked by his friends, how it was with his inward man, he replied, *I bless God I have a well-grounded assurance of my eternal happiness, and great peace and comfort within.* He gave excellent counsel to young ministers that visited him, earnestly prayed God to bless their labours, and expressed great hopes that God would do a great deal of good by them, and great joy that they were of moderate and peaceable spirits. Being at last asked how he did, his answer was *almost well*. And at length he expired, Dec. 8, 1691, and was a few days after interred in Christ Church, in London, whither his corpse was attended by a numerous company of persons of different ranks, and especially of ministers; some of them conformists; who paid him the last office of respect. There were two discourses made upon the occasion of his funeral, one by Dr Bates, and the other by Mr Sylvester. which are both in print: the former may be met with in the Doctor's *Works*; and the latter at the end of Mr Baxter's *Life* in folio.[1]

Quoting the preamble from Baxter's final Will, dated 7 July 1689, Calamy felt it to be 'something peculiar'. Indeed, it provides an amazing 'self-portrait', and deserves to be quoted in full:

> I Richard Baxter, of London, Clerk, an unworthy servant of Jesus Christ, drawing to the end of this transitory life, having through God's great mercy the free use of my understanding, do make this my last Will and Testament, revoking all other

---
1 Ibid.

Wills formerly made by me. My spirit I commit with trust and hope of the heavenly felicity, into the hands of *Jesus* my glorified Redeemer and Intercessor; and by His Mediation into the hands of God my reconciled Father, the infinite eternal Spirit, Light, Life, and Love, most great and wise and good, the God of Nature, Grace and Glory; of Whom and through Whom, and to Whom are all things; my absolute Owner, Ruler, and Benefactor Whose I am, and Whom I (though imperfectly) serve, seek and trust; to Whom be Glory for ever, Amen. To Him I render most humble thanks, that He hath filled up my life with abundant mercy, and pardoned my sin by the merits of Christ, and vouchsafed by His Spirit to renew me, and seal me as His own; and to moderate and bless to me my long sufferings in the flesh, and at last to sweeten them by His own interest, and comforting approbation, who taketh the cause of Love, and Concord as His own, etc..[1]

Being a 'great observer of providence', Baxter provided vivid examples of God's 'abundant mercy' with which He had 'filled up' his life. Indeed, says Calamy, 'he met with many surprising deliverances'.[2] These include surviving a riding accident, and being 'rescued' from gambling temptations, when he was 17. In later years, 'travelling from London into the country, about Christmas, in very deep snow, he met on the road a loaded waggon, where he could not pass by, but on the side of a bank: passing over which, all his horse's feet slipped from under him, and all the girts broke, so that he was cast before the waggon wheel, which had gone over him, but that it pleased God the horses suddenly stopped, without any discernable cause, till he got out of the way'.[3]

Baxter also recorded remarkable instances of physical healing in the Kidderminster years, in answer to the prayers of his devoted

---

[1] Ibid. p. xiii.
[2] Ibid.
[3] Ibid.

congregation: 'his neighbours set apart a day to fast and pray for him'. In particular, he suffered a tumour in his throat. 'He feared a cancer, and applied such remedies by the advice of the physician as were thought fittest, but without alteration; for it remained hard as at first'.

> At the end of a quarter of a year, he was under some concerns, that he had never praised God particularly for any of the deliverances He had formerly afforded him. And thereupon being speaking of God's confirming our belief of His Word, by His fulfilling His promises, and hearing prayers (as it is published in the 2nd Part of his *Saints' Rest*) he annexed some thankful hints as to his own experiences; and suddenly the tumour vanished ...'[1]

Another riding accident occurred at Worcester:

> The horse reared up, and both his hinder feet slipped from under him; so that the full weight of the body of the horse fell upon his leg, which yet was only bruised, and not broken: when considering the place, the stones, and the manner of the fall, it was a wonder his leg was not broken in shivers.[2]

Calamy reminds us that Baxter was not necessarily safe from danger at home, not least from his library:

> Another time as he sat in his study, the weight of his greatest folio books broke down 3 or 4 of the highest shelves, when he sat close under them; and they fell down on every side of him, and not one of them hit him, except one upon the arm. Whereas the place, the weight, and greatness of the books was such, and his head just under them, that it was a wonder they had not beaten out his brains, or done him an unspeakable mischief.

---

1 Ibid.
2 Ibid.

One of the shelves just over his head having Dr Walton's *Polyglot Bible*; all Austin's *Works*; ...[1]

As J. M. Lloyd Thomas notes, this was 'No unreal peril. Gerard J. Vossius was thus killed in his library at Amsterdam (1649)'.[2] The last of several examples highlighted by Calamy suggests the work of an assassin: 'At another time, viz. March 26, 1665, as he was preaching in a private house, a bullet came in at the window, and passed by him, but did no hurt'. Thankful Calamy thus concludes:

> Such things as these, he carefully took notice of, and recorded. And indeed his being carried through so much service and suffering too, under so much weakness, was a constant wonder to himself, and all that knew him; and what he used himself often to take notice of, with expressions of great thankfulness'.[3]

Calamy speaks glowingly of Baxter's reputation: 'Living and dying, he was much respected by some, and as much slighted by others as any man of the age'. Besides the thousands who blessed Baxter for his preaching and books, he lists the Lord Broghill, Archbishop Ussher, the Earl of Lauderdale, Sir Matthew Hale and Sir Henry Ashurst among the 'respecters'. Besides Dr Bates's account of Sir Henry's admiration for Baxter, Calamy adds that Sir Henry 'was the most exemplary person for sobriety, self-denial, piety and humility that London could glory of'.[4] Notwithstanding the later dubious reputation of King Charles II, it should be noted that His Majesty requested the publication of Baxter's sermon *The Life of Faith* (1670), before whom it was preached. As Calamy notes, Baxter 'added in the title page, By His Majesty's special Command'.[5] Needless to say, Baxter's jealous enemies challenged

---

[1] Ibid.
[2] *Autobiography*, 282.
[3] *Practical Works*, p. xiv.
[4] Ibid.
[5] Ibid. p. xv.

this claim. He also 'had many letters full of respects from eminent divines in foreign parts'. These include letters from German Lutheran Pietists[1] and such French Reformed divines as Moïse Amyraut,[2] whom Calamy also considered 'a great man'.[3]

Amyraut's letter to Baxter is significant theologically. The French theologian appreciated Baxter's affirmative remarks about him and his theology in many publications. Of course, the writings of the Saumur professor were a major source for the so-called 'middle-way' position taken by Baxter. From this perspective, Calamy narrates the suspicions entertained by the ultra-Calvinists or Owenites (or worse) towards Baxter:

> He was vehemently aspersed by those that were fond of extremes on all hands. When the lecture was set up at Pinners Hall [1672], if he did but preach for unity and against division, or unnecessarily withdrawing from each other, or against unwarrantable narrowing the Church of Christ, it was presently said he preached against such and such persons. If he did but say that the will of man had a natural liberty, though a moral thraldom to vice, and that men might have Christ and Life if they were but truly willing, though grace must make them willing; and that men have power to do better than they do, he was said to preach up Arminianism and free will.[4]

Three years later, Baxter published his major work on these and related issues—*Richard Baxter's Catholick Theologie* (1675). He persisted in propagating what he believed to be 'the Gospel Truth' to the last year of his life, including his own abridgement of *Catholick Theologie, An End of Doctrinal Controversies* (1691). Of the former work, Calamy wrote in his *Abridgement of Mr Baxter's*

---

1   See N. H. Keeble and Geoffrey F. Nuttall, *Calendar of the Correspondence of Richard Baxter* (Oxford: Clarendon Press, 1991), ii. 296 (Letter 1189).
2   Ibid. Letter 708.
3   Calamy, *The Inspiration of the Holy Writings of the Old and New Testament* (London: 1710), 201.
4   *Practical Works*, p. xv.

History, that avoiding unbiblical and ambiguous words, 'there is no considerable difference between the Arminians and Calvinists, except some very tolerable difference in point of perseverance. For which book he expected to be fallen upon by both sides, but had the happiness to escape: neither has it as I know been answered to this day'.[1]

In the biographical preface to his edition of Baxter's 'practical works', Calamy considers it inappropriate to comment further on the 'polemical works'. Quoting the commendations of Dr Bates and Bishop Wilkins already noted, he says 'I'll touch only upon those of his works that are here collected together in four volumes'.[2] Beginning with the *Christian Directory*, Calamy considers it 'is perhaps the best body of practical divinity that is extant in our own or any other tongue'.[3] We are told that *The Reasons of the Christian Religion* 'hath relieved many when under temptations to infidelity'. The *Unreasonableness of Infidelity* provides a 'clear account' of 'the nature of the witness of the Spirit to the truth of Christianity'. These apologetic works remain an antidote to the secularism which has gone from strength to strength since the seventeenth century. An added 'Discourse ... about the *Arrogancy of Reason* in opposition to divine revelation ... is very proper for those who being for a freedom of thought would know how to keep it within due bounds, so as to prevent extravagance'. This discourse also refutes the charge that since Baxter stressed the importance of reason in religion, he paved the way for a later rationalism. Indeed, biblical 'rationality' (Romans 12: 1–2; 1 Peter 3: 15) is not the same thing as 'rational*ism*', a vital distinction many still fail to draw.

Of further relevance to the 21st century, Baxter's *Reasons of the Christian Religion* provides a devastating critique of Islam.[4] Fully

---

1 *Abridgement of Mr Baxter's History*, second ed. (London: 1713), 417.
2 *Practical Works*, p. xvi.
3 Ibid.
4 See *The Reasons of the Christian Religion* (London: 1667), 202–4; also Volume 2 of Calamy's

informed of the wider events of his day, Baxter was aware of the threat to Europe posed by Islam's happily-defeated assault at the gates of Vienna in 1683. In a posthumous practical work *The Grand Question Resolved: What We Must Do to be Saved* (1692), a tract not known to Calamy (or Orme), Baxter was blunt in his estimation of Islam:

> And as you very soon discover that the religion of heathens and Mahometans is so far from shewing the true remedy that they are part of the disease itself: so you may learn that a wonderful Person the Lord Jesus Christ, hath undertaken the office of being the Redeemer and Saviour of the world: ...[1]

Calamy waxes eloquent regarding Baxter's famous *Call to the Unconverted*:

> ... which has been blessed by God with marvellous success in reclaiming persons from their impiety. Six brothers were once converted by reading it. Twenty thousand of them were printed and dispersed in little more than a year's time. It was translated into French and Dutch, and other European languages: and Mr Eliot translated it into the Indian language; and Mr Cotton Mather gives an account of a certain Indian Prince, who was so affected with this book, that he sat reading it with tears in his eyes till he died, not suffering it to be taken from him.[2]

Predictably, besides remarks on other lesser-known publications, Calamy spoke warmly of *The Saints' Everlasting Rest*: 'a book written in a very languishing condition, when in suspense of life and death: and yet it has the signatures of an holy and vigorous mind. Multitudes will have cause to bless God for ever for this book'.[3] Indeed, the book has a long and wonderful history of

---

edition.
1   Baxter, ed. A. B. Grosart, *What We Must Do to be Saved* (Liverpool: 1868), 10.
2   *Practical Works,* p. xvi.
3   Ibid.

blessing.¹ According to Dr Grosart, it was the last book read by the Duke of Wellington in 1852, 'and that within a few days of the end'.²

As for *Gildas Salvianus, or the Reformed Pastor*, Calamy says it 'perhaps contains the best model of a Gospel minister that ever was published'.³ He concludes his book comments as follows:

> I shall only add, that if the recommendations of others would have any influence upon the readers, or their characters of the author increase their esteem, few writers would have more advantage than Mr Baxter. For besides that there are none of our practical divines whose works have been translated into more foreign languages, nor are read with more admiration abroad than his; there is no one who by the fittest judges has been more applauded.⁴

Among several 'judges', Calamy quoted the famous chemist Robert Boyle (1627–91) 'who declared Mr Baxter to be the fittest man of the age for a casuist, because he feared no man's displeasure, nor hoped for any man's preferment'.⁵

Calamy's pre-penultimate testimony came from Joseph Glanville (1636–80), a Fellow of the Royal Society and later Rector of Bath. In his opinion, Richard Baxter 'was a person worthy of great respect' and that 'he was the only man that spake sense in an age of nonsense'.⁶ In an early letter to Baxter, Glanville had this to say about the eloquent Puritan's books:

> When you deal in practical subjects, I admire your affectionate, piercing, heart-affecting quickness: and that experimental,

---

1 See 'Introductory Essay' by John T. Wilkinson in *The Saints' Everlasting Rest*, Foreword by J. I. Packer (Vancouver: Regent College Publishing, 2004), 1–23.
2 Ibid. 21.
3 *Practical Works*, p. xvii.
4 Ibid.
5 Ibid.
6 ibid.

searching, solid, convictive way of speaking, which are your peculiars; for there is a smartness accompanying your pen that forces what you write into the heart, by a sweet kind of irresistible violence; which is so proper to your serious way, that I never met it equalled in any other writings.[1]

So much for Baxter's 'practical works', which many would similarly applaud. What then of the 'polemical works'? Glanvill was no less enthusiastic: 'And when you are engaged in doctrinal and controversial matters ... I find a strength, depth, concinnity [harmony], and coherence in your notions, which are not commonly elsewhere met with'.[2]

Undoubtedly saving the highest accolade for Baxter until the last, it comes from the lips of a fellow Puritan. If for Matthew Sylvester, Baxter was 'England's Elijah', and if (as endorsed by William Bates) Bishop Wilkins thought he stood alongside the early Church Fathers, Dr Thomas Manton 'declared in the hearing of several, that he thought Mr Baxter came nearer the Apostolical inspired writers, than any man in the age'.[3]

I close with quintessential Baxter, words written a few years before his death (being the very final paragraph in Dr Nuttall's biography):

> My Lord, I have nothing to do in this world, but to seek and serve Thee; I have nothing to do with my tongue and pen, but to speak to Thee, and for Thee, and to publish Thy Glory, and Thy will.[4]

After being exposed to the life and labours of Richard Baxter, I personally am left almost speechless at the display of the amazing

---

[1] N. H. Keeble and Geoffrey F. Nuttall, *Calendar of the Correspondence of Richard Baxter* (Oxford: Clarendon Press, 1991), ii. 21 (Letter 683).
[2] Ibid.
[3] *Practical Works*, p. xvii.
[4] *Richard Baxter's Dying Thoughts* (1683), 214; Nuttall, 131.

grace of God in one who may be described as the greatest Christian man England has ever produced.

SOLI DEO GLORIA

Edmund Calamy, D.D.

EPILOGUE:

BAXTER'S CHRISTIANITY

A SIMPLE SYNOPSIS

Compiled by Alan Clifford

THE WONDERFUL LOVE OF GOD

"For God so loved the world that He gave His only-begotten Son, that whoever believes in Him should not perish but have everlasting life" (John 3: 16).

O wonderful love, which condescends to such rebels, and embraces such unworthy and polluted sinners... What was the Son of God, but love incarnate? Love born of a virgin; love coming down from heaven to earth, and walking in flesh among the miserable, seeking and saving that which was lost: was it not love that spoke those words of life, those comfortable promises, those necessary precepts, those gracious encouragements which the gospel doth abound with? Was it not love itself that went preaching salvation to the sons of death, and deliverance to the captives, and offered to bind up broken hearts? Was it not love that invited 'the weary and heavy laden', and that sent even to 'the highways, and the hedges to compel men to come in, that his house may be filled?' Was it not love itself that went up and down healing diseases and doing good; that suffered them for whom he suffered, to scorn him and spit upon him, buffet him, and condemn him; that being reviled, reviled not again; that gave his life an offering for sin, died, and prayed for them that murdered him? No wonder if the gospel be it that teaches us to call God by the name of love itself, for it is the gospel that hath most fully revealed him to be so...

Directions to a Sound Conversion (1658)

THE GLOBAL GOSPEL

It is further proved by the sufferings of his Son, that God takes no pleasure in the death of the wicked. Would he have ransomed them from death at so dear a rate? Would he have astonished angels and men by his condescension; would God have dwelt in flesh, and have come in the form of a servant, and have assumed humanity into one person with the Godhead? Would Christ have lived a life of suffering, and died a cursed death for sinners, if he had rather taken pleasure in their death?

Suppose you saw him but so busy in preaching and healing of them, as you find him in Mark 3: 21, or so long in fasting, as in Matt. 4, or all night in prayer, as in Luke 6: 12, or praying with the drops of blood trickling from him instead of sweat, as Luke 22: 44, or suffering a cursed death upon the cross, and pouring out his soul as a sacrifice for our sins, - would you have thought these the signs of one that delights in the death of the wicked?

Think not to extenuate it by saying, that it was only for his elect. For it was thy sin, and the sin of all the world, that lay upon our redeemer; and his sacrifice and satisfaction is sufficient for all, and the fruits of it are offered to one as well as to another; but it is true, that it was never the intent of his mind, to pardon and save any that would not by faith and repentance be converted.

If you had seen him weeping and bemoaning the state of disobedient impenitent people, Luke 19: 41, 42, or complaining of their stubbornness, as Matt. 23: 37, 'O Jerusalem, Jerusalem, how oft would I have gathered thy children together, even as a hen gathereth her chickens under her wings, and ye would not!'

Or if you had seen and heard him on the cross, praying for his persecutors, 'Father, forgive them, for they know not what they do' [Luke 23: 34]; would you have suspected that he had delighted in the death of the wicked, even of those that perish by their wilful unbelief?

When God hath so loved (not only loved, but so loved) the world as to give his only-begotten Son, that whosoever believeth in him (by an effectual faith) should not perish, but have everlasting life', [John 3: 16], I think he hath hereby proved, against the malice of men and angels, that he takes no pleasure in the death of the wicked, but had rather that they would turn and live.

A Call to the Unconverted (1658)

THE WONDER OF JESUS CHRIST

How wonderful was the Son of God in the form of a servant? When He is born, the heavens must proclaim Him by miracles: a new star must appear in the firmament, and fetch men from remote parts of the world to worship Him in a manger; the angels and heavenly host must declare His nativity, and solemnize it with praising and glorifying God. When He is but a child He must dispute with the doctors and confute them. When He sets upon His office, His whole life is a wonder. Water turned into wine, thousands fed with five loaves and two fishes; multitudes following Him to see His miracles; the lepers cleansed, the sick healed, the lame restored, the blind receive their sight, the dead raised; if we had seen all this, should we not have thought it wonderful? The most desperate diseases cured with a touch, with a word speaking; the blind eyes with a little clay and spittle, the devil departing by legions at His command; the winds and the seas obeying His word; are not all these wonderful? Think then, how wonderful is His celestial glory? If there be such cutting down of boughs, and spreading of garments, and crying hosanna, to One that comes into Jerusalem riding on an ass; what will there be when He comes with His angels in His glory? If they that heard

Him preach the Gospel of the Kingdom, have their hearts turned within them, that they return and say, never man spake like this Man: then sure they that behold His Majesty in His Kingdom, will say, there was never glory like this Glory.

If when His enemies come to apprehend Him, the word of His mouth doth cast them all to the ground; if when He is dying, the earth must tremble, the veil of the temple rent, the sun in the firmament must hide its face, and deny its light to the sinful world, and the dead bodies of the saints arise, and the standers-by be forced to acknowledge, verily this was the Son of God: O then what a day will it be, when He will once more shake, not the earth only, but the heavens also, and remove the things that are shaken? When this sun shall be taken out of the firmament, and be everlastingly darkened with the brightness of His glory? When the dead must all arise and stand before Him; and all shall acknowledge Him to be the Son of God, and every tongue confess Him to be Lord and King? If when He riseth again, the grave and death have lost their power, and the angels of heaven must roll away the stone, and astonish the watchmen till they are as dead men, and send the tidings to his dejected disciples; if the bolted doors cannot keep Him forth; if the sea be as firm ground for Him to walk on; if He can ascend to heaven in the sight of his disciples, and send the angels to forbid them gazing after Him: O what Power, and dominion and glory then is He now possessed of! and must we forever possess with Him!

The Saints' Everlasting Rest (1650)

THE TRUTH OF CHRISTIANITY

The religion of heathens and Mahometans is so far from shewing the true remedy that they are part of the disease itself: so you may learn that a wonderful Person the Lord Jesus Christ, hath undertaken the office of being the Redeemer and Saviour of the world: and that he who is the eternal Word and Wisdom of the Father, hath wonderfully appeared in the nature of man, which he took from the virgin Mary, being conceived by the Holy Ghost: and that we might have a Teacher sent from Heaven infallibly and easily to acquaint the world with the will of God and the unseen things of life eternal: how God bare witness of the Truth by abundant, open and uncontrolled miracles: how he conquered Satan and the world, and gave us an example of perfect righteousness and underwent the scorn and cruelty of sinners, and suffered the death of the cross as a sacrifice for our sins to reconcile us unto God: how he rose again the third day and conquered death, and lived forty days longer on earth, instructing his apostles and giving them commission to preach the Gospel to all the world, and then ascended bodily into heaven, while they gazed after him: how he is now in heaven, both God and man in one Person, the Teacher and King and High-priest of his Church.

Of him must we learn the way of life: by him must we be ruled as the physician of souls. All power is given him in heaven and in earth. By his sacrifice and merits and intercession must we be pardoned and accepted with the Father: and only by him must we come to God. He hath procured and established a covenant of grace, which baptism is the seal of: Even that God will in him be our God and reconciled Father, and Christ will be our Saviour, and the Holy Ghost will be our Sanctifier, if we will unfeignedly consent; that is if penitently and believingly we give up ourselves to God the Father, Son and Holy Ghost, in these resolutions. This covenant in the tenor of it is a deed of gift, of Christ and pardon and salvation to all the world: if by true faith and repentance they will turn to God. And this shall be the law according to which he will judge all that hear it at the last: for he is made the judge of all, and will raise all the dead, and justify his saints and judge them unto endless joy and glory, and condemn the unbelievers, impenitent and ungodly, unto endless misery. The soul alone is judged at death, and body and soul at the resurrection.

This Gospel the apostles preached to the world; and that it might be effectual to man's salvation, the Holy Ghost was first given to inspire the preachers of it, and enable them to speak in various languages, and infallibly to agree in One, and to work many great and open miracles to prove their word to those they preached to. And by this means they planted the Church; which ordinary ministers must increase and teach and oversee, to the end of the world, till all the elect be gathered in. And the same Holy Spirit hath undertaken it as His work to accompany this Gospel and by it to convert men's souls, illuminating and sanctifying them; and by a secret regeneration to renew their natures and bring them to that knowledge and obedience and love of God which is the primitive holiness for which we were created and from which we fell. And thus by a Saviour and a Sanctifier must all be reconciled, and renewed that will be glorified with God in heaven. All this you may learn from the Sacred Scriptures which were written by the inspiration of the Holy Spirit and sealed by multitudes of open miracles, and contain the very image and superscription of God, and have been received and preserved by the Church as the certain word of God, and blessed by him through all generations, to the sanctifying of many souls.

The Grand Question Resolved (1692)

THE DAILY CHRISTIAN LIFE

Live daily by faith on Jesus Christ as the Mediator between God and you. Being well-grounded in the belief of the Gospel and understanding Christ's office, make use of him still in all your wants. Think on the fatherly love of God, as coming to you through him alone: and of the Spirit as given by him your head: and of the covenant of grace as enacted and sealed by him: and of the ministry as sent by him: and of all times and helps and hopes as procured and given by him. When you think of sin and infirmity and temptations, think also of his sufficient, pardoning, justifying and victorious grace. When thou thinkest of the world, the flesh and the devil, think how he overcometh them. Let his doctrine and the pattern of his most perfect life, be always before you as your rule. In all your doubts and fears and wants go to him in the Spirit and to the Father by him and him alone. Take him as the root of your life and mercies, and live as upon him and by his life; and when you die resign your soul to him that they may be with him 'where he is and see his glory.'

The Grand Question Resolved (1692)

OXFORD Academic
UNIVERSITY PRESS

Richard Baxter: *Reliquiæ Baxterianæ*

Or, Mr Richard Baxter's Narrative of the Most Memorable Passages of his Life and Times

Edited by **N. H. Keeble**, **John Coffey**, **Tim Cooper**, and **Tom Charlton**

- The first scholarly edition of this work, presenting a full and reliable text, derived from the manuscript where this is extant

- Enables an accurate understanding and appreciation of this unique early modern text and primary historical source

- Includes full supporting editorial apparatus: textual, critical, expository, historical, and literary

- Reveals the wealth of Baxter's reference to hundreds of persons (many never before identified), historical sources and texts, and contemporary events

- Accompanied by extensive general and textual introductions

Richard Baxter, ed. N. H. Keeble et al, *Reliquiæ Baxterianæ* (Oxford University Press, 2020), 5 vols. ISBN 978-0-19-959364-4, etc.

RICHARD BAXTER
The Gospel Truth

Alan C. Clifford

Alan C. Clifford, *Richard Baxter: The Gospel Truth* (Norwich: Charenton Reformed Publishing, 2016). ISBN 978–0–9929465–3–1

The chief characteristic, and main strength, of the book is its combination of commitment with scholarly rigour in setting Baxter in a wider context than is usual. Reading it, one gets a rich sense of his intellectual and religious context, his 'networks' and 'afterlife' as we say nowadays, and not only that, but the other characters in the cast list receive a respectful attention such as they do not usually attract. Alan Clifford has managed to write a book about Baxter that is individual, original, persuasive and thought provoking, distinctively his, and that is a rare thing.

Neil Keeble, Emeritus Professor of English Studies, University of Stirling

Alan C. Clifford, *Calamy Celebrated* (Peterborough, Ontario: H&E Publishing/Louisville, Kentucky: The Andrew Fuller Center for Baptist Studies, 2021). ISBN 978–1–77484–022–1

This very welcome account of Edmund Calamy has Alan Clifford's characteristic clarity and forcefulness—that is, commitment—coupled with, again characteristically, an unrivalled familiarity with the primary sources. Its summary of the context and course of Calamy's life draws out clearly his character and significance, and accords this unduly neglected figure his true place and standing in the history of dissent. The rehabilitation of Calamy's *Divine Mercy Exalted* is especially persuasive. And all this is done with a liveliness and wit too rare in scholarly writing.

Neil Keeble, Emeritus Professor of English Studies, University of Stirling

Dr Alan Clifford (b. 1941) hails from Farnborough, Hampshire. Reared in Methodism and converted in Anglicanism (1958), he embraced Puritanism through the influence of Dr D. Martyn Lloyd-Jones (1963). A career in mechanical and electrical engineering at the Royal Aircraft Establishment and the RAF Institute of Aviation Medicine, Farnborough (1958–66) was terminated after God's call to pastoral ministry. This led to university study (University of Wales, Bangor, 1966–69) and eventual ordination to the Congregational ministry (1969). Alan has pursued pastoral ministry in Northampton, Gateshead, Great Ellingham, Norfolk and is currently Pastor of Norwich Reformed Church. He remains (since 1988) a minister-without-charge of the Presbyterian Church of Wales. Academic attainments include B.A. (philosophy) 1969; M.Litt. (philosophy of religion) 1978; Ph.D. (historical theology) 1984. An in-depth study of Arminianism and Calvinism, Dr Clifford's doctoral thesis *Atonement and Justification* was published by Oxford University Press in 1990. Author of several books, articles and papers (and a few hymns) on this and related themes (including Philip Doddridge, John Calvin & the Huguenots, and the Welsh Calvinistic Methodist preacher John Jones, Talsarn), Dr Clifford has been absorbed in Baxter studies in recent years. He is married to Marian whom he met at Bangor in 1966. They have four grown-up children—three sons and a daughter—a grandson, six granddaughters and a great-granddaughter. His interests include aviation, railways, soccer (Newcastle United) and classical music (especially Buxtehude and Hummel), and currently exploring the contribution of Baxter's admiring advocate Dr Edmund Calamy.

Alan C. Clifford, *The Good Doctor: Philip Doddridge of Northampton – A Tercentenary Tribute* (Norwich: Charenton Reformed Publishing, 2002). ISBN 978–0–95267–163–3

The age of Wesley, Whitefield and Edwards was also the age of Philip Doddridge (1702–51). As a pastor, preacher, theologian, educator, author, hymn writer, philanthropist and patriot, he was a remarkable English Christian by any standard. His faithful, fragrant and far-reaching testimony to Christ made him unique in his day. This tribute introduces us to an attractive personality whose remarkable achievements merit renewed attention. At a time of confusion and uncertainty in church and society, the author believes that a rediscovery of Doddridge's contribution is long overdue.

REVIEW EXTRACTS

'A deeply interesting work about a fascinating Christian. ... the book is excellently presented, lavishly illustrated and good value for money' (*English Churchman*).

'Among other biographers ... Alan Clifford's book is now clearly indispensable. It is also warm, readable and challenging' (*News of Hymnody*).

'Lovers of Doddridge, Northampton, hymns, revival and the history of English Dissent, cannot afford to ignore this book' (*Evangelicals Now*).

Dr Clifford has ... done us a real service with the publication of his book in the 300th anniversary of Doddridge's birth. The book is well written and attractively produced. The narrative is interesting and informative' (*The Banner of Truth*).

'Doddridge's life and ministry are set out in a very readable way, and Dr Clifford's enthusiasm for his subject comes through on every page. ... [a] most valuable and stimulating tribute to one of the greatest stars in the Congregational firmament' (*Congregational Concern*).

'A scholarly and well presented book ... comprising a very useful appendix ... This book will make a valuable addition to any library and comes highly recommended' (*Our Inheritance*).

'[In] this enlightening biography ... our hearts warm to a man whose consuming desire was to win souls for Christ and whose strength and life were devoted to the glorifying of God' (*Peace & Truth*).

www.ingramcontent.com/pod-product-compliance
Lightning Source LLC
La Vergne TN
LVHW011353080426
835511LV00005B/280